ELEANOR AND DOLLY

Jenny Stafford

BROADWAY PLAY PUBLISHING INC
New York
www.broadwayplaypublishing.com
info@broadwayplaypublishing.com

ELEANOR AND DOLLY
© Copyright 2023 Jenny Stafford

Cover art by Brandi Underwood

First edition: November 2023
ISBN: 979-8-88856-000-6

Book design: Marie Donovan
Page make-up: Adobe InDesign
Typeface: Palatino

ELEANOR AND DOLLY received development and support from the Boulder Ensemble Theatre Company, Athena Project, Vintage Theatre, and Des Moines Area Community College.

ELEANOR AND DOLLY received its original production at Temple University in Philadelphia opening on 14 September 2023. The cast and creative contributors were:

Ellie	Eliana Pinckney
Jana	Zoe Necowitz
Claire	Ontaria Kim Wilson
Liam	Roman Fosco
Mrs. Speare	Isabella Phillips
Clerk	Shannon Mohan
Police Officer	Olivia Brown
Understudy	Jacob Challenger
Director	Brandon McShaffrey
Associate Director	Yana Vilchynskaya
Scenic design	April Thomson
Costume design	Jenna Grove
Lighting design	Liam Shaffer
Sound design	Darren West
Head of Props	Lindsey Silver
Stage Manager	Faith DeShields
Dramaturg	Brandi Underwood

Special thanks to Fred Duer, Robert Stroker, Brandon McShaffrey, Rob Hartmann, and Temple University.

CHARACTERS & SETTING

ELLIE, *eighteen, female. A high school senior. Intelligent, organized, ambitious, tightly wound.*

CLAIRE, *mid-thirties, female.* ELLIE's *mom. Fun-loving, free-wheeling, bohemian; an embracer of life.*

JANA, *eighteen, female.* ELLIE's *best friend. Sarcastic, funny, irreverent.*

LIAM, *eighteen, male. A Canadian exchange student. Quiet, mousy, withdrawn and a bit dull.*

CLERK/MRS SPEARE/POLICE OFFICER, *late forties/early fifties, female.*

A small town in Indiana. 2014.

A note on production: The locations in this play can be minimalistic and representational in terms of scenic design. The original production found that in using the balloons, placing a piece of clear tape over the balloon and pricking it with a pin achieved the desired slow deflation.

NOTE ON MUSIC

For performance of copyrighted songs, arrangements
or recordings referenced in this play, permission
of the copyright owner(s) must be obtained. Other
songs, arrangements or recordings may be substituted
provided permission from the copyright owner(s) of
such songs, arrangements or recordings is obtained,
or songs, arrangements or recordings in the public
domain may be substituted.

Dedication: For Lindsay, the Jana to my Ellie.

Scene One

(ELLIE, 18, sits at a desk in a pristine room. She, herself, is pristine and put together. She writes in a notebook.)

ELLIE: I am the top veterinary ophthalmologist in Chicago. *(Beat. She continues to write.)* I am both my high school and college valedictorian. I own apartments in Paris and New York. I—

(From behind her bed, her friend JANA pops up, chewing gum and making a cat's cradle out of yarn.)

JANA: This doesn't make any sense.

ELLIE: What?

JANA: None of that's true. You're just like…lying.

ELLIE: It's not lying. It's a strategy. You have to write down your goals as if you have already achieved them. And then your brain chemicals shift around and start to believe it, and then you start behaving like the person you want to become. If I write down that I am the top veterinary ophthalmologist in Chicago, then I start to believe I am the top veterinary ophthalmologist in Chicago. Then I start to *act* like the top veterinary ophthalmologist in Chicago, and by acting that way I become—

ELLIE & JANA: —the top veterinary ophthalmologist in Chicago.

JANA: So it's like…*The Secret.* You Secret it.

ELLIE: I secrete what?

JANA: No, like, you put it out into the universe, and summon it to you.

ELLIE: Eew, no! That's like, weirdo magic bullshit. *(She holds up the journal.) This* is real.

JANA: And you do this every day.

ELLIE: Every. Day. I made my list of my life goals, and I write them down every morning.

JANA: Jeez. What are you, forty and having a midlife crisis?

ELLIE: Nope. I'm taking a page from Eleanor Roosevelt.

JANA: Ugh. You and Eleanor Roosevelt. Eleanor Roosevelt told you to do this?

ELLIE: In a way. She says—

(ELLIE *grabs Eleanor Roosevelt's* You Learn By Living *off a shelf.)*

JANA: No! Do not read that thing to me again!

ELLIE: "The purpose of life is to live it, to taste experience to the utmost, to reach out eagerly and without fear for the newer and richer experience."

JANA: …and from that you got "write down your goals maniacally?"

ELLIE: The "newer and richer experience" doesn't just happen. You have to make a plan. That's what Eleanor did.

JANA: Yeah, every morning she got up and wrote, "Be born rich, marry my cousin, ride nepotism to the top."

ELLIE: Or, you know, "Chair the United Nations Human Rights Commission. Write seventy-eight books. Organize Marian Anderson's Lincoln Memorial concert to promote black women and protest racism. *In 1939.*"

JANA: This is what you're writing down?

ELLIE: No. I have my own goals. But I've hit a snag with one of them. You have to help me.

JANA: You want *my* help? *You're* Ellie Hoyt. *I* once put a towel in the microwave, trying to make a homemade heating pad after I sprained my ankle when I tried to karate kick my own shadow on the wall, and then the towel caught on fire and I couldn't run for help because of my ankle, and my parents had to renovate their kitchen. *(Beat)* I'm just saying, I don't know if I can help.

ELLIE: You can. Okay. Listen. Here's the list of goals. Number one. I am the top vet—

JANA: No. Skip forward. Number four, or wherever we left off.

ELLIE: Fine. But two is high school and college valedictorian—high school I'll be able to check off in May. College will be a few more years, but I'm on track for that too. Three, I own apartments in Paris and New York. If I'm crushing the others, I'll be on track for that. Number four… *(She looks at number four. She pauses.)* Number five, I—

JANA: What's four?

ELLIE: We don't need to worry about that one. Number *five*, though, is—

(JANA *jumps up and tries to grab the journal out of her hands.)*

JANA: What's four?! I wanna see four!

(ELLIE *manages to keep the journal way from her.* ELLIE *shouts over her.)*

ELLIE: Number five! I married my high school sweetheart!

(Beat)

JANA: What?! Who are you dating?! Why didn't you tell me?!

ELLIE: No one!

(ELLIE *drops her head onto her desk. Beat.*)

JANA: No one.

ELLIE: *(Muffled, with her head on the desk)* No one.

JANA: Well…you're screwed.

ELLIE: No! You have to help me!

JANA: We graduate in three months. We've known all the same small-town loser boys since kindergarten. It's over. Cross this one off.

(JANA *reaches for a pen to scratch it out, and* ELLIE *leaps across the room to stop her.*)

ELLIE: No! Don't touch it!

JANA: As a feminist, I'm embarrassed for you that this one is even on here. *(She holds up the book with Eleanor Roosevelt's face on it.)* Eleanor Roosevelt judges you.

ELLIE: I'm a feminist too. It's not anti-feminist to want to get married. I know that that's one of the things I want in my life. So I wrote it down.

JANA: Okay. So go to vet school and marry some hot piece there. Don't marry any of the losers from our school.

ELLIE: Jana, look at this list. Look at all the massive goals I have ahead of me. I can't be distracted by men. I can't spend years dating. And I can't risk getting murdered by some Tinder killer. I need someone in the bag.

JANA: In the bag?!

ELLIE: You think I'll have time to sort through men AND ace vet school? No. I can't risk getting derailed from my other goals because my focus is divided. I don't have to *marry* him now, I just have to *find* him now.

JANA: Or…you just don't achieve this one. It's not like the world will burn down like a microwave towel fire.

ELLIE: No. Chronologically, this is the first goal on my list. Even before valedictorian. *(Beat. With desperation)* If I *start* my life with a goal I can't achieve…it's just going to pull at the thread, and the whole sweater of my life is going to unravel.

(ELLIE is interrupted by her mom, CLAIRE, entering her bedroom. She's in her late thirties, with a free, breezy, boho style to her. She runs in holding a phone.)

CLAIRE: Look at this one! Look at this one! Look at this one!

ELLIE: *(Focused on her journal)* Dog or man?

(CLAIRE gives her a playful shove and holds out her phone.)

CLAIRE: PUPPY! Look at his little face! Look at his little ears! Look at his nose!

ELLIE: Yep, those are all the components of a puppy.

(JANA crowds over to see.)

JANA: I love him. I want him now. Bring him to me.

CLAIRE: His name is Beauregard, and he's a cocker spaniel mix, and—

ELLIE: Mom. We've been over this. Puppies are a lot of work. You have to feed them, and train them, and clean up after them. And who's going to end up doing all of that? *Me.*

CLAIRE: Hey! I kept you fed and clothed and alive for eighteen years. And I'd say I did a pretty good job, right?

(ELLIE makes a noncommittal sound and returns to her journal.)

CLAIRE: Anyway. I'll sleep on Beauregard.

ELLIE: Yes, you will. You will roll over on him in your sleep and kill him. Beauregard will be beau-re-dead in a month.

CLAIRE: What are you doing tomorrow night?

CLAIRE & ELLIE: Studying.

CLAIRE: Well, blow that off, and let's go to Sandy's new pottery painting place. We can get dinner first. Six o'clock?

ELLIE: Is Jerry coming?

CLAIRE: No! *(Pinching her cheeks playfully)* Not to our weekly mother-daughter date! Plus, Jerry's over.

ELLIE: Dead or dumped?

CLAIRE: Dumped. Maybe dead. Who knows after you dump them, right?

ELLIE: Bummer. He was smarter than some of the others.

CLAIRE: Psh. He was duller than *all* of the others. Life's too short. Jana, write that down.

JANA: Write what down?

CLAIRE: The wisdom I'm imparting to you. "Life is too big and beautiful and wonderful to be bored. And if you're bored, it's your own fault."

JANA: I don't have a pen.

(CLAIRE *stands to go.)*

CLAIRE: Stitch it on a pillow. I'm out. Pottery? Tomorrow night? Six?

ELLIE: *(Teasing)* I thought life was too short to be bored.

CLAIRE: *(Teasing back)* Gasp! You've turned on me. *This* pottery won't be boring—I'm gonna paint something raunchy on a platter.

(CLAIRE *exits. A moment.*)

JANA: God, your mom is so cool.

ELLIE: Can we get back to my problem?

JANA: Like, I feel like your mom is the kind of mom that wouldn't care if you set a microwave fire.

ELLIE: She wouldn't, because she'd be the one *setting* the fire. *(Beat)* I think she suddenly woke up and realized I'm going to college in the fall, and feels the need to cram in like, eighteen years of bonding in the next few months.

JANA: So, bond with her. She's awesome.

ELLIE: Jana, *who am I going to marry?*

JANA: Why do you think I can help you with this?

ELLIE: Because you're like…*good with boys*. You can talk to them. I just feel weird and awkward, so I'm thinking maybe I overlooked someone.

JANA: A) You didn't. And B) What are you talking about? You're…fine with boys. You've had boyfriends. Colin Douglas.

ELLIE: We dated for one day in fifth grade before he changed his mind.

JANA: And everyone else is—

ELLIE: Mean.

JANA: Or—

ELLIE: Stupid.

JANA: Or—

EllE & JANA: Taken.

ELLIE: That's all the boys in town.

JANA: Your mom has had like a million boyfriends. Where does she find all her guys?

ELLIE: Online, and most of them are from other towns. They're like, weekend relationships.

JANA: Ask her about it then! You probably need an online non-townie too.

ELLIE: Yeah, because she's found love with so many winners. It's ok. I'm going to keep brainstorming. Every problem can be solved, and I am going to solve this one.

JANA: How?

(Beat. ELLIE writes in her journal.)

ELLIE: "I have solved the problem of finding my high school sweetheart."

(JANA sighs and flops back on the bed. Blackout.)

Scene Two

(The next night. A pottery studio. ELLIE and CLAIRE sit at a table with small pots of paint and brushes, each holding a blank piece of pottery. CLAIRE has the promised platter, and ELLIE has a mug.)

ELLIE: Are you really going to paint something raunchy on that? Because I will leave.

CLAIRE: I haven't decided yet! The platter is my oyster. What are you going to paint?

ELLIE: I don't know. I looked up an idea on Pinterest earlier, but it was for a bigger mug. Now I don't know what to do.

CLAIRE: You'll figure it out. *(She starts haphazardly slapping paint on the platter.)*

ELLIE: You don't want to like, sketch it out in pencil first?

CLAIRE: Nah, that's no fun. So…how's school?

ELLIE: It's good. I have an AP bio exam tomorrow. I feel pretty good about it though. How's work?

CLAIRE: Ugh. I keep telling Greg that we need to order more interesting beads—every bead we have would get stitched on a granny shawl. If we want younger, more artsy people to shop there, we have to stock bolder stuff. Why would artisanal jewelry makers come to our store, when flippin' Michaels in Mishawaka has a better supply than we do?

ELLIE: I mean, that's a nice idea, except that no one would drive to this town just for art supplies. Or any reason at all, actually.

CLAIRE: They would if we could make it like, a cool destination shop and we had stuff no one else had! Like these. (*She gestures to her own bold, colorful earrings.*) Remember when we drove to Santa Monica to get the beads for these?

ELLIE: Oh, you mean that time you unexpectedly picked me up from fourth grade in the middle of the day and we drove for thirty-one hours with no plan whatsoever?

CLAIRE: Yes! That was a great trip!

ELLIE: Yeah—it was great when we ran out of gas… or when we had to sleep in the car in the Walmart parking lot.

CLAIRE: But then we finally got there, and we spent *hours* in those bead shops. Oh! And we ate that clam chowder on the pier—

ELLIE: Oh yeah! And we rented the tandem bike and went on the whale watching tour—

CLAIRE: —and the guy! Remember the guy!

(ELLIE *bursts out laughing, and* CLAIRE *and* ELLIE *mimic his voice:*)

CLAIRE & ELLIE: "We probably won't see any whales today."

CLAIRE: But then we saw that, um, gray one—

ELLIE: —the humpback! And a blue whale, and a minke whale!

CLAIRE: And the dolphins! That whole herd—

ELLIE: —pod—

CLAIRE: Of dolphins!

ELLIE: They were beautiful. Ok, that was a fun trip.

CLAIRE: Let's do that again! Let's go tomorrow!

ELLIE: *(Laughing)* Mom, I have my AP Bio test. I told you.

CLAIRE: I'll call you in sick and you can take it next week! I've got the itch now, and if we overthink it we won't go. Come on!

ELLIE: Mom, I'm not in fourth grade anymore. You can't just kidnap me and take me along on your whims. I'm an adult. I have responsibilities.

CLAIRE: Psh. So what? I'm an adult with responsibilities too!

ELLIE: *(Laughing in spite of herself)* Okay.

*(A tense two seconds—what could turn into a much bigger moment is interrupted when a saleswoman [*CLERK*] comes over.)*

CLERK: How are we doing over here? *(She looks at* CLAIRE'*s very colorful platter.)* Oh my, I love that! Such bold colors!

CLAIRE: Thanks, Sandy!

(The CLERK *looks at* ELLIE'*s mug.)*

CLERK: Oopsie! You forgot to paint something!

ELLIE: I'm just having a hard time deciding what to paint.

CLERK: *(Like she is speaking to a very small child)* Well, I know you like animals. So you could paint a dog? Or a cat? Or a lion? Or an elephant? Or—

CLAIRE: A *pod* of elephants.

CLERK: Ooh, what's that?

ELLIE: It's a *herd* when it's elephants. It's like a family of elephants. They travel together, and protect each other. They hunt for food as a team. They're really social.

CLERK: *(Still as if* ELLIE *is a small child)* Wow, you know a lot about elephants! You should be a trainer at the zoo!

ELLIE: No, I'm going to the University of Chicago to get my BS in Animal Biology in the fall. I just got my acceptance letter last week.

CLERK: Well, wow! So fancy! *(To* CLAIRE*)* You must be awfully proud! Didn't you go to Chicago too?

CLAIRE: Well, I *almost* went to the Art—

ELLIE: She didn't go anywhere.

(An uncomfortable beat)

CLERK: Well, let me know if you need any help!

(The CLERK *exits, and* ELLIE *and* CLAIRE *give a little laugh.)*

ELLIE: Was she like…explaining what animals are to me?

CLAIRE: "A dog, or a cat, or a raccoon, or a ferret—"

(They laugh again.)

CLAIRE: That's cool about the elephants. Being a family. *(Beat)* So do the baby elephants stay in the…herd… with their parents forever or what?

ELLIE: Well, the dad isn't usually in the picture.

CLAIRE: Preach it, sister.

ELLIE: —but some female elephants stay with their moms their whole lives, in the same herd.

(Beat)

CLAIRE: We should start wrapping up—I have a date later tonight.

ELLIE: You do? With who?

CLAIRE: Some guy. Nate, maybe?

ELLIE: Online guy?

CLAIRE: Yeah—he seems nice enough. We'll see.

ELLIE: Is…um…do you get nervous? Meeting men? Like…talking to them?

CLAIRE: Nah. It's like, I am who I am, he is who he is, and we just see if we click. It's fun! Either way, you get to meet a new person. Hear someone's story. It's a good time. Boobs or butt?

ELLIE: What?

(CLAIRE *holds up her very colorful platter, which has two curved lines painted in black over top of it.*)

CLAIRE: Boobs or butt? It could go either way. If I leave it, it's a butt. If I add nipples, it's boobs.

ELLIE: Eew, Mom. Neither.

CLAIRE: *(Shouting across the store)* Hey, Sandy!

(*The* CLERK *returns.*)

CLAIRE: Boobs or butt?

CLERK: Oh, my. Um…one of each?

(CLAIRE *adds one nipple.*)

CLAIRE: Nah, too Picasso. Boobs it is. Nipples all around.

(CLAIRE *adds a second nipple and hands the platter to the* CLERK.)

CLAIRE: Fire away. Ellie?

(ELLIE *hesitates, then hands her blank mug to the* CLERK.)

CLERK: You didn't paint anything!

ELLIE: Decision paralysis, I guess. Fire away.

CLERK: You want me to…

ELLIE: Just…dip it in the stuff and fire it. It's…snow. It's a cloud. It's…blank.

(*Beat*)

CLERK: Alrighty then.

CLAIRE: Nah, wait. (*She takes the mug and quickly paints two curved lines on it.*) Butt. (*She holds it up next to the platter, delighted.*) Now they're a set!

Scene Three

(*The next day. School.* ELLIE *stands at her locker with her backpack, organizing things. The inside of her locker is decorated with pictures and quotes by Eleanor Roosevelt.* JANA *comes scurrying up to her.*)

JANA: Oh my God, oh my God, oh my God you won't believe what's happening.

ELLIE: What?

JANA: We got a foreign exchange student.

ELLIE: What?

JANA: And it's a guy.

ELLIE: What?!

JANA: Fresh meat! You secreted fresh meat!

ELLIE: Stop! Eew! What are you talking about?

JANA: Nick told Scott who told Allie who told Kristen who told *me* that Max's family is getting a foreign exchange student for the rest of the year.

ELLIE: Where is he from?!

JANA: I don't know.

ELLIE: What year is he?

JANA: I don't know.

ELLIE: When is he getting here?

JANA: Why aren't you asking any of the right questions?! Is he hot? Is he single? Is he a good kisser?

ELLIE: Is he?

JANA: I DON'T KNOW! *(She points to a picture of Eleanor Roosevelt on* ELLIE'S *locker.)* I can't believe this worked. I'd go for him myself, but I think I'd be like, interfering in whatever pact you have going on with the ghost of Eleanor Roosevelt. By the way, take these down. This is weird. Put up posters of hot shirtless guys like a normal person. Jeez.

ELLIE: I can't believe this. This is even better than I could have planned it! And I plan everything! A foreign guy?! They're so…sophisticated and sexy. What if he's from France? What if he speaks French? And one of my goals was to—

ELLIE & JANA: —own an apartment in Paris!

JANA: *Stop it!!!* I'm getting a journal and starting this secreting bullshit tomorrow.

ELLIE: Okay, we need to calm down. Every girl in school is going to go for him. I'm not going to stand a chance.

JANA: I have a feeling you are.

ELLIE: Why's that?

JANA: Because…

(MRS. SPEARE enters.)

MRS SPEARE: Ellie. I need you to show a new kid around.

JANA: Bing!

ELLIE: Of course! I'd be happy to!

(MRS SPEARE is in her late forties. She looks exhausted, and carries a comically large coffee cup. She glances at a crumpled paper in her hands.)

MRS SPEARE: He's a foreign exchange student. His flight is delayed so he won't get here until lunch, so just stop by the office and pick him up on your way.

ELLIE: Where is his flight delayed from?

MRS SPEARE: No idea.

ELLIE: Do you know if he's—

MRS SPEARE: *(Holding up the paper)* Here's what I know. "Tell Ellie to pick up the FES." And if you can, try to dissuade him from engaging in the activities that happen in the equipment closet and behind the staircase in B hallway.

JANA: *(Before she can stop herself)* You know about that?

MRS SPEARE: I know about everything. That's why I didn't ask *you* to show him around. If anyone can keep him on the straight and narrow, it's Ellie.

ELLIE: Oh, well. I don't know. I'm still…like, a rabble-rouser, ya know?

(MRS SPEARE and JANA chuckle.)

MRS. SPEARE & JANA: Okay.

MRS SPEARE: Nice locker. *(She starts to exit.)* Oh! I have a feeling I know the answer to this, but have you decided who you're going to be? For the living history exhibit?

ELLIE: Oh. Well… *(She gestures awkwardly towards her locker, and the pictures of Eleanor Roosevelt.)*

MRS SPEARE: Smart lady. Going for that scholarship, eh? *(She raises her coffee cup and exits.)*

JANA: Ellie! Why do you refuse to give yourself any advantages in life? Look, I know how you feel about her, but *this* is who you want to look like at the living history exhibit? In front of the whole school? Look at her!

(ELLIE and JANA look at the locker. She is, in fact, not exactly photogenic.)

JANA: Help yourself out. Pick Dolly Parton or someone. Except don't, because that's who I'm doing.

ELLIE: Jana! Dolly Parton isn't going to win you the scholarship!

JANA: Please. This whole thing is a charade; everyone knows you're going to win it. So I might as well look hot up there. You should try it.

ELLIE: Hey! Eleanor knew she wasn't pretty and it plagued her her whole life, and I'm going to talk about that and how society disvalues brilliant women based on their looks.

JANA: Wow. What a great way to die a virgin. Speaking of which, it's almost lunch and we need to go pick up your foreign lover so you can picnic on the Seine and he can feed you grapes while he reads you French poetry.

(ELLIE and JANA squeal with excitement.)

ELLIE: He might not be French. Maybe he's from somewhere else romantic. Spain, or Germany…

JANA: Or fleeing some war-torn country and you can nurse him back to health…

ELLIE: Or he's a deep, brooding Italian…or his family owns an elephant sanctuary in Thailand—

JANA: What?

ELLIE: Wherever he's from, I'm ready. I'm conversational in five languages, and my romantic future husband has been delivered to my front door because *I willed it to happen.* I—

*(A very average-looking young man [*LIAM*] walks up behind them.)*

LIAM: Hi, is one of you Ellie?

ELLIE: Um, I'm Ellie. Who are you?

LIAM: I'm Liam. I'm the new foreign exchange student? I got here earlier than they thought, so they told me where your locker was, and said you'd show me around?

*(*ELLIE *and* JANA *exchanged confused/panicked looks.)*

JANA: Of course she will. Where are you from, Liam?

LIAM: Canada!

(Blackout)

Scene Four

(Later that day. In the lunchroom. ELLIE, JANA, *and* LIAM *sit together.* JANA *looks at* LIAM *warily.* ELLIE *looks at him optimistically.)*

ELLIE: How's your macaroni and cheese?

LIAM: My what?

ELLIE: Your macaroni and cheese?

*(*LIAM *looks at his lunch.)*

LIAM: Oh, my kraft dinner? It's fine. Not as good as at home.

JANA: That's probably because you poured ketchup all over it.

LIAM: Do you not do that here?

ELLIE: Excuse her, she's in a mood today. That's sooo interesting. *(She flirtatiously tucks her hair behind her ear, and it gets stuck in a tangle. A brief, awkward struggle as she tries to continue breezily.)* So what part of Canada are you from?

LIAM: Ottawa. It has been voted the most boring city in Canada.

*(*JANA *drops her head into her hands and moans.)*

ELLIE: *(Trying way too hard)* Well, I bet our town could give you a run for your money. If you're seeking adventure…the middle of Indiana is not it. That's why Indiana Jones always confused me. He's like, the epitome of adventure, but he's named after the most boring state, with the most generic last name. I mean, *legally* his first name is Henry. Henry Jones. *(Beat)* Jr. *(Proudly)* Not a lot of people know that. But his *adventure* name is Indiana, which I guess he gave himself, or might have been the name of his dog, which totally doesn't—

*(*JANA *can take no more and jumps in to cut* ELLIE *off and save her.)*

JANA: Soooo, why did you come here, Liam? Why are you here?

ELLIE: What Jana means is—this is a…surprising place to come as a foreign exchange student…with only a couple of months left of the year?

LIAM: I don't know. Seemed fun.

JANA: It's not.

LIAM: Just wanted a change of pace. Change of scenery. One last chance to get an impressive thing on my university applications, I guess.

ELLIE: Oh! Where are you going to college?

LIAM: I'm not sure yet.

ELLIE: What do you want to study?

LIAM: I'm still deciding.

(JANA *looks at* LIAM *quizzically, trying to figure him out.*)

JANA: Were you like, the bad boy of Ottowa, and your parents sent you to this dead town to try to tame you?

LIAM: *(He smiles a little)* Ha, no. Honestly, not a lot of places accept exchange students mid-year. So…here I am.

(JANA *sighs, then perks up.*)

JANA: Wait. They speak French in Canada, right?!

(JANA *and* ELLIE *exchange hopeful eye contact.*)

LIAM: A lot of people do.

ELLIE: Oh?

LIAM: I don't.

JANA: Oh.

(Trying to change the subject:)

LIAM: So. Are you guys going to university?

JANA: Undecided.

ELLIE: I'm going to the University of Chicago. I'm going to study animal biology.

LIAM: Wow. You must like animals.

(Beat)

ELLIE: I do.

LIAM: Do you like cats?

ELLIE: The animal?

(A long beat)

LIAM: Yeah.

ELLIE: *(Panicked)* I was just checking, because there's also a musical called—

(A school bell rings.)

LIAM: Hey, can you tell me where room 206 is?

ELLIE: Oh. I'll walk you there!

LIAM: That's ok. If you point me in the right direction, I'm sure I can figure it out.

ELLIE: Sure. It's that way, then take a left.

LIAM: Thanks so much. *(Beat)* See you around.

(LIAM picks up his lunch tray and exits. JANA has covered her face with her hands overlapping, and watched the previous exchange through the gaps in her fingers.)

JANA: Gaaaah. Waffle fry hands. I had to watch that through waffle fry hands.

ELLIE: *(With disbelief)* "The animal?" He says, "do you like cats," and I said, "*the animal*?!"

JANA: Eh, who cares. This isn't your guy.

ELLIE: Henry Jones Jr.?! Why am I such a disaster?

JANA: Ellie, this guy is dry toast. He came from the most boring city in Canada to the most boring city in America to put ketchup on his macaroni and cheese.

ELLIE: But—

JANA: Look, he's not hot. He's not exciting. He didn't even say "eh" at the end of any of his sentences, which is really all I'm looking for from Canadians. Abort this mission. Find a hot guy in college.

ELLIE: No! You can't just give up when it's not easy right away! *(Beat. Deflated)* I don't get it. For everything else in my life, I can make a strategic plan. But I get all turned around and I suck at guys, and…feelings, and…chemistry. And I'm awesome at chemistry.

JANA: Hey. You were only half responsible for the epic train wreck that just happened.

ELLIE: And now, if I can somehow turn this situation around, *that's* the story we're going to have to tell our kids about how we met. How mom accidentally brought up Andrew Lloyd Webber like an idiot.

JANA: Stop it. I stand by my original thought. This whole plan was stupid. Because you're the smartest, most awesome person I know, and that milk-toast loser is making you feel like shit about yourself. Screw 'im.

ELLIE: *(Not convinced)* Thanks. I've got to go. I'll see you later. *(Upset, she gathers up her lunch tray and bag and exits.)*

Scene Five

(That afternoon. ELLIE dejectedly walks in the door, home from school. CLAIRE is working on a beading project on the couch. ELLIE drops her bag and flops into a chair.)

CLAIRE: Oof. Rough day?

ELLIE: The worst. I'm a failure.

CLAIRE: I doubt that. This will cheer you up. Look at this one! *(She holds out her phone.)* Bad day, get a puppy. I really think we should move fast on this one. She's not going to be a puppy forever.

ELLIE: Mom, you have to think it through.

CLAIRE: By the time I think it through she won't be a puppy anymore! She'll just be some full-grown dog! Who wants that?

ELLIE: What do you think is going to happen to it after you adopt it?!

CLAIRE: *(Looking at the puppy, talking in a baby voice)* Oh, you're just so cute aren't you?! *(She turns the phone to* ELLIE, *doing a puppy voice.)* Please give me a home and lots of love! I'll cheer you up every day!

ELLIE: Mom. I'm telling you, you really have to give it some thought. Maybe start with a fish.

CLAIRE: I started with a daughter, and I gave that no thought at all. And it was the best thing that ever happened to me. *(Beat)* I don't mean I gave it no thought at all. I mean I didn't plan it out ahead of time. I mean I—

ELLIE: Nope. Stop. You don't have to go any further.

CLAIRE: I'm just saying that if you overthink everything, you'll think yourself out of every great experience in your life. This thing that happened today that made you all mopey—did you overthink it?

(Beat)

ELLIE: Maybe.

CLAIRE: There ya go. Want to talk about it?

ELLIE: I'm okay. Thanks, though.

CLAIRE: Okay. I'm gonna make dinner.

*(*CLAIRE *crosses to the kitchen and starts cooking.* ELLIE *remains on the couch, wrapping herself in a blanket and moping. Several moments of silence pass.* ELLIE *turns something over in her mind. Then--)*

ELLIE: Hey mom?

CLAIRE: Yeah?

ELLIE: You were eighteen when you had me, right?

CLAIRE: Yep.

(Beat)

ELLIE: So…I guess you got some guy…my dad…to fall in love with you when you were in high school, huh?

CLAIRE: Ha, no. I got some guy to have sex with me in high school. These are not the same. And PS, one star. Do not recommend.

ELLIE: *(With increasing speed and desperation)* So were you like…high school sweethearts? Did you get him to ask you on a date? Did you talk on the date? Like, what did you talk about? What do people talk about?!

(Beat. CLAIRE *comes over from the kitchen holding a spoon.)*

CLAIRE: What's happening?

ELLIE: Nothing.

CLAIRE: …are you pregnant?

ELLIE: *(Losing it)* What?! No! *(In despair) How would that ever happen?!*

CLAIRE: I don't understand what's happening. Is there…a guy?

ELLIE: No. Yes. I don't know.

*(*CLAIRE *dramatically drops her cooking spoon and sits on the couch by* ELLIE.*)*

CLAIRE: I knew this day would come. I knew that someday, *someday,* you'd look up from one of your books and there would be a guy, and you and I would finally have something to talk about.

*(*CLAIRE *playfully pulls* ELLIE *to her.)*

CLAIRE: Come into my bosom.

*(*ELLIE *laughs a little, in spite of herself.)*

ELLIE: Mom! Stop. Come on. We talk about lots of things.

CLAIRE: Sure, but basically since you learned to read and were tall enough to reach things, you haven't really needed me. But this! *This* I can help you with!

ELLIE: You…want to help me?

CLAIRE: I always want to help you. Ok. Tell me everything.

ELLIE: He's a foreign exchange student.

CLAIRE: Ooooh—

ELLIE: *(Cutting her off)* No, no. From Canada.

CLAIRE: Eh, whatcha gonna do. So he's cute?

ELLIE: He's okay.

CLAIRE: He's funny?

ELLIE: Not particularly.

CLAIRE: Then he's rich?

ELLIE: Not that I can tell…

CLAIRE: What are we doing here?

ELLIE: I just…I want to have a chance with him. That's all. And I'm so awkward. I just say all the wrong things.

CLAIRE: Well, what does he say?

ELLIE: "Goodbye", mostly.

CLAIRE: Like, what was his part of the conversation?

ELLIE: I don't know. Not much. I guess I did most of the talking.

CLAIRE: Bingo. There's your problem. You've got to make *him* do the talking.

ELLIE: How?

CLAIRE: In my experience, everyone has at least one thing they're really passionate about, and can talk about forever. So you've just got to ask him questions until you unlock it. That's what I—

ELLIE: Wait, you're right!

CLAIRE: I know I am. That's what I—

ELLIE: No, stop, hold on!

(ELLIE *frantically digs through her backpack and pulls out Eleanor Roosevelt's* You Learn by Living. *She flips to a page and begins reading.*)

CLAIRE: Oh. Good. This book again.

ELLIE: "I made a game of trying to make people talk about whatever they were interested in. Ruth Bryan Rohde once told me that she found it very useful, if she was sitting next to a person whose interests she knew nothing about, to begin going through the alphabet. A is for ants. 'Mr. Jones, are you interested in the life of the ant?' He might not be interested in the ant, but at least he was startled and amused." THAT'S IT! She's a genius.

CLAIRE: That's…literally what I suggested.

ELLIE: I've got it. I can make a plan now. I have to go make a list! (*She grabs her stuff and heads to her room.*)

CLAIRE: Okay. Well, dinner will be ready soon.

ELLIE: I'll eat it in my room! Thanks mom!

Scene Six

(*The next day, at school.* ELLIE *and* JANA *sit at a lunch table.*)

JANA: This isn't going to work.

ELLIE: It's totally going to work. LIAM!!!

(ELLIE *screams across the lunchroom to get* LIAM'*s attention, as he stands with his lunch tray. He jolts, startled, then gives a small smile and makes his way over to them.*)

JANA: (*Under her breath*) I can't believe I have to watch this two days in a row. (*Perking up as he approaches.*) Hi, Liam! We were afraid you made new friends and wouldn't want to sit with us today.

LIAM: Ha, no, not since yesterday.

ELLIE: Well, I'm glad. You can sit with us anytime. What's for lunch today?

LIAM: Pizza. And this cardboard box of milk. The spout disintegrates when you drink it. It makes no sense.

JANA: What do you use in Canada? A glass bottle?

LIAM: No, a bag.

JANA: A *bag*? A bag of milk? Like, "I'll just have a bag of milk, please?"

LIAM: It works much better.

JANA: A bag of milk is an udder. A cow's udder.

ELLIE: Jana, you have to be open to other cultures.

JANA: IT'S A COW'S UDDER! (*She takes a breath.*) Okay. I'm sorry. Continue.

(*A long moment of silence as they each take a bite of their lunch.* ELLIE *gives* JANA *a knowing look, and takes a deep breath. She is about to put her plan into action.*)

ELLIE: So, Liam. Do you like…aardvarks?

LIAM: Aardvarks? Is that also a musical? Like the cats?

JANA: Now see, *that* I would watch.

ELLIE: No, just like, the animal. Aardvarks.

LIAM: I…sure. I don't really know anything about them.

(ELLIE *slyly crosses "aardvarks" off a list in her lap, and checks for the next thing.)*

ELLIE: I just finished this really interesting book about the Bermuda Triangle.

LIAM: That sounds interesting.

(Beat)

ELLIE: It was. *(A moment. She crosses "Bermuda Triangle" off her list.)* We already covered cats. Divorce! Do you know anyone who's divorced?

LIAM: Everyone knows someone who's divorced.

ELLIE: Care to expand on that?

(Beat)

LIAM: No thank you.

(Lights shift to indicate the passage of time. They come back up on the same table, but JANA *is now resting her head on the table.)*

ELLIE: Monks.

LIAM: *(Perking up)* What did you say? Monkeys?

ELLIE: *(Eagerly)* We can talk about monkeys!

LIAM: I'd rather not. My uncle fell into a monkey pit at the zoo. It didn't end well.

ELLIE: So…monks?

(Lights shift to again indicate the passage of time. They come back up on the table, this time JANA *is lying on the lunch table bench with her head hanging off the back of it.)*

ELLIE: Rasputin. There's an evil guy.

(Beat. LIAM *takes a bit of his pizza, looking perplexed. Lights shift to indicate the passage of time. When they come back up on the table,* JANA *is now lying on the floor, using her backpack as a pillow.)*

ELLIE: …and every zebra has totally unique stripes, that scientists can actually scan like barcodes to keep track of them.

(JANA *pops her head up.*)

JANA: Is that true? They scan them?

ELLIE: It is!

JANA: That one's actually cool.

(*From her spot on the ground,* JANA *slaps* LIAM *on the leg.*)

JANA: Hey Liam! That one was cool!

LIAM: Yeah. Zebras. I mean, are they white with black stripes, or black with white stripes, right?

JANA & ELLIE: Black with white stripes.

JANA: Don't they have Google in in Canada?

(*The lunch bell rings. They start to gather their things;* ELLIE *looks dejected. Her plan didn't work.*)

JANA: Peace out.

ELLIE: Well, thanks for having lunch with us. It was great. (*She starts to walk away.*)

LIAM: I…um…I watched *Cats* last night.

ELLIE: What?

LIAM: *Cats.* The musical. (*Beat*) I didn't get it.

ELLIE: No one gets it. That's like, its thing.

LIAM: Would you want to like, come over and watch it tonight? Maybe as a future vet—

ELLIE: —ophthalmologist.

LIAM: —you would have insights that make it understandable.

ELLIE: (*Stammering*) Um, yeah. I would love that.

LIAM: Great. I'll find you after school.

(LIAM *exits, and* ELLIE *stands for a moment in disbelief.*)

ELLIE: EEEEEE!

Scene Seven

(*Later that night,* ELLIE*'s house.* CLAIRE *and* JANA *sit on the couch talking worriedly when* ELLIE *walks through the door.* CLAIRE *and* JANA *leap to their feet.*)

CLAIRE/JANA: Where have you been?/You're not dead!

CLAIRE: Jana and I have been worried sick! Where were you? Are you okay?

ELLIE: I'm fine! Calm down! I come home this late all the time and you never even notice!

CLAIRE: To be fair, I didn't notice this time. But even Jana didn't know where you were! If you're going to be late, you need to text Jana!

JANA: I need to know where you are at all times! I thought you were dead!

ELLIE: No, my phone is dead. I—

JANA: I checked all your spots. My house, the library, your house. You weren't at any of them! Where were you?

ELLIE: (*Blushing*) I…um…I was at Liam's house.

(*Beat.* CLAIRE *and* JANA *look at each other.*)

CLAIRE: I'll get the wine.

JANA: We're eighteen. Get popcorn.

(JANA *tackles* ELLIE *to the couch, and* CLAIRE *and* JANA *sit very close to her on either side.*)

JANA: Shut. UP. But start talking. What happened? When I left lunch we were explaining Google to him and he was a hopeless case!

CLAIRE: Was this like…a *date*?

ELLIE: Um….I don't know. Jana, after you left he invited me over to watch *Cats*.

CLAIRE: Is that what they call it now? You were safe, right?

ELLIE: No, like, we watched *Cats*. The musical.

JANA: What is happening.

CLAIRE: Okay, so you watched *Cats*. But like, what did you talk about? Did you sit close together? Was there hand holding? Was there a kiss?

ELLIE: There was none of that. He's not that talkative, and I went through the alphabet again. Alps through zygotes.

JANA: And did he try anything?

ELLIE: No, he just sat on the other side of the couch. Which I'm kind of glad for, because I think I would have freaked out if he tried anything.

CLAIRE: So it was a great first step. You're getting to know each other. And now you've established a relationship where you hang out outside of school.

ELLIE: Unless it *wasn't* a date and it was just like… a friend hang. I don't know. This is all really confusing.

CLAIRE: Welcome to dating. Maybe you're just taking it slow. That's fine!

ELLIE: I can't take it slow! I don't have time to take it slow!

CLAIRE: What's the rush?

(ELLIE *and* JANA *look at each other—is* ELLIE *going to tell her mom about the list?*)

JANA: Prom. Ellie really wants a date for prom and it's next month, so she's got to get cracking.

CLAIRE: You're going to go to prom?! Like we can go dress shopping and I can do your hair and take a picture of you with a boy and pretend to wait up worried all night?!

ELLIE: Well, I mean…I guess people go to prom with their high school sweethearts, right? I guess that would be a good next step.

CLAIRE: Oh, I'm so excited. Last year on prom you made me watch that documentary on earth worms with you.

ELLIE: Hey! *World of Worms* was good!

CLAIRE: I'm so happy to see you branching out! Being a human teenage girl! Okay. So what's the plan? How are we going to get him to ask you to prom?

JANA: Hello, it's not 1950. She could ask him.

CLAIRE: Hello, I'm in my thirties. Check yourself.

JANA: I'm just saying. How did you get him to watch *Cats* with you? W-werd? *(Beat)* W-W-E-R-D?

(ELLIE and CLAIRE look confused.)

JANA: What would Eleanor Roosevelt do?!

ELLIE: Oh no, Eleanor Roosevelt. I'm supposed to meet with Mrs Speare about my living history project, and I didn't do any of the stuff she asked me to do! This is why men are a mistake—I wasted a whole evening over there and now I'm behind and—

JANA: *(Looking at her phone)* Shut up. While you were talking I googled "How to Get a Guy to Ask You to Prom". Clearly Eleanor Roosevelt can't help you here.

CLAIRE: I thought she was asking him.

JANA: Look at her. She's a mess. We'll save it as a last resort.

ELLIE: Come on. This is so dumb. *(Beat)* What does it say?

JANA: It's a twelve-step list. Ellie, you love lists! And at the end of this article is a link to another article with suggested Instagram captions for photos on prom night.

CLAIRE: Dear God.

JANA: Okay.

*(*JANA *stands* ELLIE *up and spruces her up—fixing her hair, grabbing a new cardigan off a nearby chair and changing her outfit, etc. She then turns* ELLIE *around and pushes her to the other side of the stage, where* LIAM *sits at a lunch table. The scene is now a split scene—on one side,* JANA *and* CLAIRE *sit on the couch reading out the list, and on the other side,* ELLIE *and* LIAM *are at the lunch table as* ELLIE *tries out the ideas.)*

JANA: Here we go. "Number one. Befriend him." You already did that—we're gonna fly through these! "Number two. Flirt with him."

ELLIE: Oh God.

JANA: "When you're with your crush, try to be noticeably warm and present."

*(*ELLIE *looks back at* JANA *nervously.)*

JANA: GO!

*(*ELLIE *nervously approaches the lunch table.)*

ELLIE: Hi, Liam! I had such a great time at your house. Thanks for inviting me over.

LIAM: Sure! It was really fun.

(Beat. ELLIE *leans in a little too close.)*

ELLIE: So…tell me all about your day.

JANA: "Make strong eye contact. Hold eye contact longer than you would with other friends, and gaze deeply, with intention."

(ELLIE *opens her eyes way too wide, unblinking, and leans into* LIAM. *He scootches away, and* ELLIE *and her bug eyes scootch closer again.*)

LIAM: Um…I went to Spanish, and Geometry, and—

JANA: "Keep your feet and torso planted towards him."

(ELLIE *awkwardly adjusts her body into a very unnatural position.*)

JANA: "And find ways to innocently touch him when he says something funny."

ELLIE: *(Hissing to* JANA *from her awkward position)* He never says something funny!

JANA: You've just have to make *him* think he's funny!

LIAM: Ellie? Are you okay?

(ELLIE *laughs a little too hard.*)

ELLIE: Am I okay?! I'm more than okay. I'm spectacular!

(ELLIE *reaches over and grabs* LIAM'*s arm in a death grip.*)

LIAM: Ow!

ELLIE: *(Dropping all her mannerisms)* Oh my gosh, I'm so sorry. Are you—

LIAM: I…um…I forgot I'm supposed to…

(LIAM *makes a run for it.* ELLIE *crosses back to* JANA *and* CLAIRE.)

ELLIE: Well, that went great. This is the dumbest thing I've ever done.

(CLAIRE *leans in teasingly with intense bug eyes.*)

CLAIRE: How was your day?

(ELLIE *laughs.*)

ELLIE: Mom, shut up!

JANA: Look, that was only the beginning. Would Dolly Parton give up?

(*Beat*)

ELLIE: I don't know. Are you seriously studying Dolly Parton for your project?

JANA: I am and she wouldn't!

ELLIE: She wouldn't have to; what guy would turn her down?! I can't do any more of this.

JANA: Yes you can!

(JANA *shoves* ELLIE *back over to the lunch table; it's a new day. She gives* CLAIRE *the phone.*)

JANA: Read the next one.

CLAIRE: Why are we taking advice from the internet? You know you have a *mom* who's got some experience in this area and could help out.

JANA: Sure, but like…are you married? I'm just saying.

(CLAIRE *gives* JANA *a playfully evil glare.*)

CLAIRE: I thought I liked you. Okay. "Step three. Recognize his signs of flirting."

(LIAM *enters with his lunch tray.*)

CLAIRE: "Does he smile every time he sees you?"

(ELLIE *waves at* LIAM, *and he gives the world's smallest smile, which could easily be interpreted as a nervous smile after yesterday.*)

ELLIE: He did! He did! He did!

(LIAM *sits at the table.*)

CLAIRE: "Read his body language. Is his gaze pointing at you?"

(LIAM *keeps his gaze on his sandwich.*)

CLAIRE: "Are his feet pointed towards you?"

(LIAM *shifts so his feet are pointing the opposite direction.*)

CLAIRE: "Does he have straight posture?"

(LIAM *is very hunched over his sandwich.*)

CLAIRE: "Does he have open body language—no crossed arms or legs?"

(*As* LIAM *eats, he crosses both.*)

ELLIE: (*Whispering across to* CLAIRE *and* JANA*)* No! No to all of this! He has the body language of a dead butler at a haunted mansion! Should I touch him again?

CLAIRE & JANA: No!

CLAIRE: Move to the next step! "Drop hints. Talk about how excited you are for prom. Some examples of things you can say are, 'I wonder what kind of music they'll play at prom,' or 'I can't wait to see my friends in their dresses,' or 'I just know this prom is going to be memorable.'" (*She turns to* JANA.) Whoever wrote this isn't married, either.

(*Focus shifts back to* ELLIE *and* LIAM.)

ELLIE: So…do you guys have prom in Canada?

LIAM: Yeah—we call it a formal though.

ELLIE: We call it prom, which is short for promenade. Like, a parade of everyone looking really good, I guess. (*Beat. Forced*) I can't wait to see my friends in their dresses.

LIAM: Won't you have a dress too?

ELLIE: Of course. I mean, if I go. I don't know who I'm going with yet. I am…available.

CLAIRE: Hey, that was the next step! "Mention you're available."

ELLIE: Are you…going to prom?

LIAM: I don't know yet. I don't really have anyone to go with.

(Beat)

ELLIE: Huh. So…you don't have anyone to go with, and I don't have anyone to go with.

(Beat. The lunch bell rings.)

LIAM: Well, gotta go to class. See you later, El. *(He takes his lunch tray and exits.)*

JANA: That boy is as dumb as a bag of milk.

ELLIE: He called me "El!" He gave me a nickname! I hate it, but it's a nickname! *(Beat)* I don't get it. I gave him the perfect opening, and he didn't ask.

CLAIRE: Sometimes it takes guys a while to summon their courage. You laid the ground work—now he'll be thinking about it! Go slow!

ELLIE: Prom's only two weeks away now! *If* I pull this off, I'll need time to find a dress. Find a hairdo. Make a list of conversation topics for the night.

CLAIRE: I'll help you. It will be fine.

JANA: She's right though. We've got to accelerate this. *(She takes the phone.)* "Write him an anonymous note that says, 'Someone wants to go to prom with you.'" Then, "ask a friend to put in a good word for you." BINGO! Here we go. Stand aside and watch the master.

(CLAIRE stands up and straightens her clothes and starts to head to the lunch table. JANA and ELLIE both grab her and force her back on the couch.)

JANA: Not you!

CLAIRE: It said have a friend put in a good word! I'm good with men!

ELLIE: You're not my friend, Mrs Robinson, you're my mom. Jana, go.

(JANA *does some neck circles and cracks her knuckles, and heads over to the lunch table. Lights go down on* ELLIE *and* CLAIRE—*they don't see the next part.* LIAM *sits at the table.)*

JANA: Sup, Montreal.

LIAM: Ottawa.

JANA: Whatever. I brought you something. (*She pulls a small ziplock bag of milk out of her hoodie pocket.*) It's a bag of milk. So you'll feel more at home.

LIAM: This isn't really how that works.

JANA: Flip it over.

(LIAM *flips the bag over and reads a message written on the bag in sharpie.)*

LIAM: "Someone wants to go to prom with you." I'm not sure what to do with this.

JANA: Well, A) I wouldn't drink it 'cuz it's been in my pocket since like seven this morning, but B) use the brain your Canadian God gave you.

LIAM: Wait. I saw this on YouTube. This is like, a "promposal", right?

JANA: Well—

LIAM: Okay. Sure. I'll go with you!

(*Blackout*)

(*Optional Intermission*)

Scene Eight

(Later that day, after school. JANA sits on her bed, looking in a hand mirror, attempting to tease her hair. We hear a voice from offstage.)

JANA'S MOM: *(Offstage)* Jana? You'd better be practicing for the living history performance!

JANA: *I AM! JEEZ!*

(JANA sighs deeply and makes a pained face. She holds up her phone and attempts to push "play" several times, but can't bring herself to do it. Finally she takes a deep breath and quickly hits the button before she can overthink it. The first notes of Jolene, by Dolly Parton, plays. JANA stands and begins practicing her lip-synch performance, but it is hitting very close to home.)

JANA: Jolene, Jolene, Jolene, Jolene…
I'm begging of you, please don't take my man…

(Music fades outs.)

Scene Nine

(ELLIE sits in MRS SPEARE's classroom.)

MRS SPEARE: So you don't have the timeline.

ELLIE: No.

MRS SPEARE: Or the early years biography.

ELLIE: Not *written down*, but I know all about her early yea—

MRS SPEARE: And you don't have your costume sketch.

ELLIE: Again, not on paper, per se, but I can—

MRS SPEARE: What's going on, Ellie?

ELLIE: Nothing. I've just been busy.

MRS SPEARE: This isn't like you. And need I remind you this isn't just a school project; this is a scholarship competition.

ELLIE: I know it is.

MRS SPEARE: You're about to graduate. This isn't the time to sit back and slack off. You need to think about your future.

ELLIE: *(Snaps)* I do! I am! *All I do is think about my future! (Beat. She is visibly upset.)* I'm sorry. I'm really sorry.

(MRS SPEARE organizes some papers on her desk and hands ELLIE a tissue.)

MRS SPEARE: Anything you want to talk about?

ELLIE: No.

MRS SPEARE: This wouldn't have anything to do with the new guy, would it?

(ELLIE ponders for a moment, and then everything spills out.)

ELLIE: I have this list of goals for my life, and one of them is to marry my high school sweetheart. And I don't have one. And then Liam came and it seemed like maybe I could cross that goal off too, but it's so hard. And I feel so turned around and somehow this became all I think about, and I'm running out of time, and if I fail this I'm pretty sure it's just going to be a domino effect and I'm going to fail everything in my life just like my mo— *(She stops herself.)* I just…I can't fail at my first goal.

(Beat)

MRS SPEARE: What else is on your list of goals?

ELLIE: *(A little embarrassed)* Um…I want to be the top veterinary ophthalmologist in Chicago. I want to be my high school and college valedictorian. I want to

own homes in New York and Paris. There's…there's
another one.

(MRS SPEARE *takes a sip of her coffee.*)

MRS SPEARE: I married my high school sweetheart. Did
you know that?

ELLIE: *(Flatly)* No. Congratulations.

MRS SPEARE: We met junior year. I was planning on
going to USC, but he didn't get in there, so we decided
to both go to a smaller college near our hometown,
and we got married our sophomore year there. When
we graduated I was offered a teaching fellowship in
London, but we had just bought a house—well, our
parents helped us buy a house—and with the mortgage
payments, we couldn't afford for me to cover the costs
associated with the fellowship. So I stayed and taught
at the local high school. I worked my way up and they
were eying me to be principal there, and he got a job
here, which was a great opportunity for him. More
money than we were making there. So we moved here,
and I started over at this school. *(Beat)* Once you get
married, it's not all about you anymore—you don't
get to call all the shots in your life. I love my husband
with all my heart. He's made sacrifices for me too. But
sometimes I wonder what would have happened if I'd
gone to USC. If I'd done that fellowship in London.
If I became principal. *(Beat)* You're a smart girl, Ellie.
You'll make the right decisions for you. But it's worth
considering that if you achieve this first goal, you
might not be able to achieve some of the others.

(ELLIE *ponders this for a moment. The bell rings and she
gathers her papers.*)

MRS SPEARE: We'll meet next week. Try to have more of
this project under your belt by then, eh?

ELLIE: I will. Thanks, Mrs Speare.

(ELLIE *exits the classroom and bumps into* JANA, *who is carrying two balloons and is on her way into* MRS SPEARE'*s room.)*

ELLIE: Jana! I've been looking everywhere for you!

JANA: I'm meeting with Mrs Speare about my Dolly Parton project.

ELLIE: What are the balloons for?

(JANA *holds them up in front of her like breasts.)*

ELLIE: Oh my God.

JANA: What? I've been researching her for this project, and she's actually really cool! At first I just wanted to dress up like a whore--which it turns out is *literally* what she *intentionally* based her look on--but she's like a smart businesswoman, and a philanthropist, and—

ELLIE: Okay, I can't take you seriously with those things. *(She pushes the balloons back down.)* Which is probably what everyone said to Dolly Parton.

JANA: You're being like, super judgmental. The more I study her, she's like, becoming *my* Eleanor Roosevelt.

ELLIE: You did not just say that. Look, did you talk to Liam? Did you drop the hint?

JANA: Um, yeah, about that. The situation took a bit of a turn. There's good news and bad news.

ELLIE: What does that mean?

JANA: I…um…I debated even telling you this, but Dolly Parton says to be honest. I dropped the hint, and he misunderstood it because he's a moron, and…he asked me. To prom.

ELLIE: *What?!* Why would he want to go with you? You're so mean to him!

JANA: *I know!* I said no, obviously.

(ELLIE *sits on the ground and leans against a locker.)*

ELLIE: Well, of course. Of course he'd rather go to prom with Dolly Parton than Eleanor Roosevelt.

JANA: What does that mean?

ELLIE: Just…you know what I mean.

JANA: I'm not sure I do.

ELLIE: You've been around, okay? You're a staple in B Hallway. And he probably knows it.

JANA: Wow. What are you saying, I'm a slut, and that's the only reason someone would want to go to prom with me?

ELLIE: No, I—

JANA: Because by the way, I don't know if you've noticed, but I also don't have a date for prom, and I've been spending all my time and energy helping *you* get one. And you've never even asked me about me.

ELLIE: Jana, I—

JANA: But you know what? I could just take your guy, since *he asked me*. But I'm not going to do that because I'm not some kind of…*Jolene*.

ELLIE: I don't even know what that means.

JANA: I don't want to go with just any old loser who comes along.

ELLIE: Oh really? Is that what you think I'm doing?

JANA: It *is* what you're doing! And you know what, you can still do it! That's the good news part! I told Liam no, and I told him to ask you. And since you'll both just go with whoever comes along, apparently, it's a perfect match.

ELLIE: Look, is Liam awesome? No. Is Liam interesting? No. Is Liam an embarrassment to Canadians everywhere? I don't know, I haven't met that many Canadians, but I'm guessing he is. But I—

(JANA *gives* ELLIE *a glare and subtle point, and* ELLIE *whirls around to see that* LIAM *is standing behind her.)*

ELLIE: Oh. Liam. I—

(LIAM *turns and exits.)*

ELLIE: Oh, my God. (*She starts to follow him.)*

JANA: Oh, so we're just done here? That's the person you're going to run after?

ELLIE: I have to fix this. I'll talk to you later!

(ELLIE *exits.* JANA *sighs, then holds up her balloon breasts again. At some point during the fight, one of the balloons deflated significantly, and the effect is really sad.)*

JANA: Awww, man.

Scene Ten

(A bench outside of school. LIAM *sits on the bench, and* ELLIE *approaches cautiously.)*

ELLIE: Liam, I'm so sorry. I didn't mean any of those things.

LIAM: Well, you said them behind my back, so I think you did mean them. I thought we were friends.

ELLIE: We *are* friends.

LIAM: You know, it's *so hard* being here. Away from my life. Away from my parents. Trying to unlearn the metric system. And I was so happy I had made at least one friend to get me through to graduation. But I didn't. (*He stands up to leave.)*

ELLIE: Okay. Um…I'm just going to be really honest here. I only said those things because I was upset that you asked Jana to prom, and not me.

LIAM: I didn't ask Jana to prom. She asked me. With a ziplock bag of sour milk.

ELLIE: She was supposed to be letting you know that *I* wanted to go with you.

(LIAM *chuckles.*)

LIAM: She did not do a good job.

(ELLIE *lets out a small laugh too.*)

ELLIE: She did not. But then you agreed to go with her, so I was upset, and I said all those terrible things, and I'm really sorry.

LIAM: I didn't want to go with her. I was just caught off guard and didn't know how to say no.

ELLIE: Come on. Jana's like, beautiful.

LIAM: She's one of the scariest people I've ever met.

(ELLIE *laughs.*)

LIAM: Look…I wanted to go with you too.

ELLIE: You did?

LIAM: Yeah. I read this internet article about how to ask a girl to prom—

ELLIE: *(Nervous laughter)* That's so dumb.

LIAM: —and I was doing all of it, and you were *not* taking the bait.

ELLIE: Um…what were you doing?

LIAM: It said to ask you on a date first, so I did. I watched *Cats* two nights in a row for you.

ELLIE: So it *was* a date.

LIAM: And I sat there on the other side of the couch all night, waiting for you to make a move, and nada. And then the article said to not be too eager—that I should hang back and not talk too much and play hard to get.

ELLIE: You did that *really* well.

LIAM: So…um…I guess…*do* you want to go to prom? Together?

(ELLIE *nods.*)

ELLIE: Yeah. I do.

(LIAM *smiles, and* ELLIE *and* LIAM *sit in silence for a moment.*)

LIAM: Do you ever feel like…you don't actually want to *go* to prom? Like, you just don't want to go the rest of your life with people asking you about your prom, and then looking at you really sadly when you say you didn't go?

ELLIE: *(With a huge sigh of relief)* That's *exactly* how I feel. *(Beat)* But I think if my mom finds out I got a date for prom and then I don't go, she'll disown me.

LIAM: Yeah, my mom's the one who sent me that article.

ELLIE: Is it hard being away from your parents for so long?

LIAM: It's fine. I should get going. We'll figure out details and stuff, okay?

(LIAM *waves and exits.* ELLIE *sits on the bench a moment, and* JANA *walks by with her backpack.*)

ELLIE: Jana! Jana, wait!

JANA: I have to go, Ellie.

ELLIE: Jana, look, I'm sorry. I—

JANA: Did you fix your perfect future with Liam?

ELLIE: I guess so. We're going to prom together. The plan is back on track.

(JANA, *deadpan, mimes throwing confetti on* ELLIE.)

JANA: Confetti. *(She starts to walk away.)*

ELLIE: Wait! You could go with us!

JANA: Ha! No thank you.

ELLIE: Not like, a throuple or something. Just like, a group of friends.

JANA: I don't need your pity! I got a date!

ELLIE: In the last half hour?

JANA: I forgot to take my balloons out of my shirt after my meeting with Mrs Speare and Jed, from the baseball team, asked me. Even though one of them had deflated.

ELLIE: Oh, Jana! Don't go with Jed! He's such a total—

JANA: There it is again! You are nothing but judgement, Ellie!

ELLIE: It's a well-known fact that he's a douche.

JANA: Well if he's a douche and I'm a slut, it should be a perfect pairing, huh?

ELLIE: Look, I said I was sorry—

JANA: Well it's too little too late! You've made too many little comments like that for it to just magically be okay, Ellie. *(Beat)* I always knew that people—like my mom, or Mrs. Speare, or people at school—judged me that way. It was always really nice that *you* didn't. But I guess you've secretly thought that all along, huh?

ELLIE: Come on, Jana! I know you! You do not *want* to go with Jed, and—

JANA: Well you know what I've thought all along? You can be a judgmental bitch. Maybe I'm gonna go with Jed because I *want* to go with Jed. I have a lot of options, actually—I'm not desperate like you.

(Beat. That one hurt. ELLIE's eyes narrow. She is ready to strike back.)

ELLIE: Yeah, I bet you *do* have a lot of options.

JANA: I'm sure you and Liam will have a great time. *You're so much fun.* Try not to let him know that he could have been literally anyone, and you'd still have used him to check a box on your list.

(JANA *whirls around and exits.* ELLIE *slams her backpack and exits the other way.*)

Scene Eleven

(*A dress shop.* CLAIRE *sits on an ottoman, waiting for* ELLIE *to come out of a dressing room.*)

ELLIE: (*Offstage*) Eleanor Roosevelt said that you should always own a black dress, because no one ever remembers a black dress.

CLAIRE: Well, that is *not* what we are going for. Come out and let me see!

ELLIE: This…I hate this one. I'm going to put on the black one.

CLAIRE: No, let me see the one I picked first!

(ELLIE *steps out of the dressing room in a tight, short, brightly colored dress with a plunging neckline. She self-consciously tries to cover herself up.*)

CLAIRE: Ellie! You look gorgeous!

ELLIE: Nope. Nope. I can't wear this! What do you think Liam is going to think if I show up wearing this? This is going to send the wrong message.

CLAIRE: You know, this actually reminds me of my prom dress a little bit, and—

ELLIE: Well, that seals the deal. Hard no.

(ELLIE *turns to enter the dressing room to take it off.*)

CLAIRE: Wait, wait, wait! Wear it until Jana gets here! She'll be on my side with this. You'll see.

ELLIE: Jana's not coming.

CLAIRE: Why not?

ELLIE: We're kind of…in a fight. I don't know.

CLAIRE: You and Jana? About what?

ELLIE: Nothing. It's stupid. *(Beat)* She said I'm judgmental and not any fun. I'm fun, right?

CLAIRE: Well…

ELLIE: Ugh, never mind. And I am *not* judgmental. I have to get out of this dress; my IQ is dropping.

(ELLIE enters the dressing room, eventually hanging the short flashy dress on a hanger outside the dressing room. CLAIRE and ELLIE talk as she changes.)

CLAIRE: And what did you say?

ELLIE: *(Offstage)* About what?

CLAIRE: Fights have two sides. Jana said you're not fun. What did you say?

ELLIE: *(Offstage)* I don't know. I said she's…*too* fun. With guys.

CLAIRE: Ellie!

ELLIE: *(Poking her head through the curtain)* I know, I know. And I don't even care about that—she can do what she wants! I was just already mad and it felt like an easy stab.

CLAIRE: Well, you've got to fix this with her.

ELLIE: *(Offstage) She said I'm not fun!*

(ELLIE bursts through the curtain wearing a floor-length black dress. Very modest. It's not fun.)

CLAIRE: Now why would she say that?

ELLIE: What do you think?

CLAIRE: Well, it's…pretty?

ELLIE: I know! And look—doesn't it look just like the one Eleanor Roosevelt is wearing in her fireplace portrait?

(ELLIE *pulls it up on her phone and shows* CLAIRE.)

CLAIRE: Wow. She is just…deeply unattractive, isn't she?

ELLIE: That doesn't matter.

CLAIRE: I know it doesn't but…this is an official portrait? Like, this is the best they could do for her?

(ELLIE *pulls her phone away.)*

ELLIE: I think she looks nice. And I think I do too.

CLAIRE: Of course you do. I'm just saying, you're an eighteen year-old girl, and you have the rest of your life to dress like a first lady of… *(She looks at the photo again.)* …indeterminate age. And this dress is— *(She glances at the price tag.)* —whoo! Are we sure we don't want to look at a different dress?

ELLIE: Mom, look, this night is really important to me. Like, *really* important. I need everything to go perfectly.

CLAIRE: I know that when you're in high school prom seems like the most important thing, but in the grand scheme of things—

ELLIE: This *is* the grand scheme of things. All of this is steps to the grand scheme of things. This is the dress I need to be in that night. I can feel it.

CLAIRE: Well, can we also live in it and eat it? Because it's like a month's rent.

(Beat)

ELLIE: Some people pay a lot more than this for rent. People that live in nicer places. Some people don't even pay rent, they pay mortgages.

CLAIRE: …Okay?

ELLIE: I have some money saved up for college; I can dip into that maybe and help. Since I'm also paying for my own college. Somehow.

CLAIRE: Okay, let's watch ourselves, Ellie. I said I would pay for your prom dress, but we need to be reasonable.

ELLIE: This is reasonable! For lots of people, this is reasonable!

CLAIRE: Well for us it's not, ok?

ELLIE: Well, whose fault is that?

(A moment. JANA *enters, looking at* ELLIE's *dress.)*

JANA: Yikes, who died?

ELLIE: Jana, what are you doing here?

JANA: My mom and I were just at Dillards getting my prom dress. She tried to dress me in a snuggie and a chastity belt. *(She walks over to the short, flashy dress on the hanger, and turns to* CLAIRE.*)* Did you pick this dress?

CLAIRE: Maybe.

JANA: Because it's awesome.

CLAIRE: Thank you! Would *you* like to be my daughter?

JANA: I *wish. (She looks* ELLIE *up and down.)* Is that the dress you're getting?

*(*ELLIE *looks at* CLAIRE.*)*

CLAIRE: Yeah. That's the one she's getting. I'm gonna— *(She holds up her phone.)* —move some money around. *(She steps back away from the girls, onto her phone.)*

JANA: What was that?

ELLIE: Nothing. Why did you come over here, Jana? Just to give me crap about my dress?

(JANA *looks over her shoulder to make sure* CLAIRE *is out of earshot*).

JANA: No. I have some news I thought you'd be interested in.

ELLIE: What?

JANA: Jed and some of the guys from the baseball team got a bunch of hotel rooms for after prom. And since you're *so fun*, I hooked you and Liam up with one of the rooms.

ELLIE: For…why?

JANA: We need one more couple to split the bill. But also for sex, dummy.

ELLIE: *What?* With Liam?! I barely know him! I haven't even kissed him!

JANA: Well then logic it out for me, because you've been trying to marry him, and that's a lot bigger deal than this. You can sleep with hundreds of guys in a lifetime, but you can only marry…a few.

(Beat)

ELLIE: But I've…I've never…with anybody.

JANA: Well, I can almost guarantee you that he hasn't either. If you're each other's firsts, it will bond you for life.

ELLIE: I don't know…you'll be in one of the hotel rooms?

(CLAIRE *starts to head back over to them, but stops and listens—they don't see her.*)

JANA: Ah, I knew you wouldn't let that slip by. What? Afraid if you do this you won't feel like you're better than me anymore? Be young. *Be fun*, grandma! It's just prom. It's just hotel rooms. It's just sex.

(CLAIRE *freezes at this, then jumps into action.*)

CLAIRE: Okay, let's go. I moved some monies, I'll sell some stuff on ebay. Let's go check out.

ELLIE: Really? I can get this dress?

CLAIRE: Yep, let the Eleanor Roosevelt cosplay commence. Ellie, get changed, let's go. I'll meet you at the register.

ELLIE: Okay, I just—

CLAIRE: Now.

(CLAIRE *exits.* ELLIE *and* JANA *exchange a "what's her problem?" look.* ELLIE *heads to the dressing rooms to change.)*

Scene Twelve

(*Prom night.* ELLIE *sits in the living room in her dress;* CLAIRE *is doing her hair. Both seem a little on edge.)*

CLAIRE: What time is he getting here?

ELLIE: 6:30. We need to hurry a bit, okay?

CLAIRE: I'm almost done! (*She does a finishing flourish.)* There! Take a look at *that*!

(CLAIRE *hands* ELLIE *a mirror.)*

ELLIE: Wow—that is….big.

CLAIRE: Don't worry, it won't look so big once I do your makeup.

ELLIE: I already did my makeup.

(CLAIRE *squints and looks at* ELLIE*'s face.)*

CLAIRE: Okay, but you need like, *evening* makeup. Prom makeup. Don't worry, I have a whole plan! (*She pulls out a bag of makeup and starts rifling through it. A moment)* So…how are you feeling about tonight? Excited?

ELLIE: Mmm-hmm.

CLAIRE: What…are you most excited for?

ELLIE: I don't know. Dancing and stuff.

CLAIRE: Cool. *(Beat)* Oh, hold on! I have something for you!

(CLAIRE runs offstage; ELLIE stands and paces, shaking out her hands and rolling her neck to try to calm her nerves. CLAIRE returns with a jewelry box.)

CLAIRE: Here.

ELLIE: What is this?

CLAIRE: I made them for you! At the shop! Earrings and a necklace!

(ELLIE warily takes the box and opens it. From her face we can tell that she doesn't like them.)

ELLIE: Wow! That is…so nice of you. Thank you! *(She puts the box aside.)*

CLAIRE: No, they're for tonight! I know after the dress we couldn't really afford more for jewelry, so…I made your prom jewelry!

ELLIE: Oh! I just…I don't know if it really goes with the dress, you know?

CLAIRE: Of course it does. I waited until you picked your dress so I could match it. Put it on!

(CLAIRE takes the necklace and stands behind her, putting it on her. It's big and bulky, and feels suffocating. ELLIE twists away.)

ELLIE: Mom, stop, it's so big.

CLAIRE: You just have to let me clasp it and—

ELLIE: *(Exploding)* No! Stop! I don't want to wear this!

CLAIRE: *(Also frustrated)* Will you let me do *one thing* for you, Ellie?

ELLIE: You didn't do this for me! This is a "you" necklace!

CLAIRE: I made it *for* you—

ELLIE: No, you didn't! You made it for you, as usual! Just like you tried to get me to wear *your* dress, and have *your* hair, *your* makeup, *your* jewelry! Just stop! I don't want to be *anything* like you!

CLAIRE: You've made that very clear. I'm sorry you hate everything about me, and about the life I've tried to build for us!

ELLIE: What life?! This whole night is about ensuring that my life doesn't turn out like yours *at all*!

CLAIRE: Hey! I have been doing the best I can with what I have!

ELLIE: I'm sorry, but everything about our life is disorganized and chaotic and unstable! I can't wait to get out of here!

CLAIRE: Oh, I'm well aware! I wish you would show a little gratitude, Ellie—even once.

ELLIE: I wish you would have looked at that picture of the dress, known how much I liked it, and tried to make jewelry that looked like the jewelry in the picture. I wish you would get to know who I am, instead of constantly trying to change me.

CLAIRE: I'm not trying to change you! But you are wound so tightly that you are going to turn your whole life into one big to-do list, and you are going to miss your life, Ellie!

ELLIE: Well, having lists is how you don't end up living in some dumpy town, making second-rate jewelry, floating from man to man to man—with no dreams and no goals and no plan!

CLAIRE: Gee, I wonder how Jana could have called you judgmental?!

(CLAIRE *crosses to* ELLIE'*s backpack and pulls out* You Learn By Living. *She holds it up.*)

CLAIRE: I read this. You think I'm not trying to get to know who you are? I read this, trying to find some way to get inside your head. Some way to connect with you. And you know what I found? This whole book is Eleanor Roosevelt telling you to seize life, and have adventures. It's about being interested in other people. Interested in learning. Open to joy. You've missed the point of this book.

ELLIE: No I haven't.

CLAIRE: Yes, you have! You have such a one-track mind that you don't even get to spend prom with your best friend! You're pushing away everyone around you, and using this book as the reason…and you totally missed it. (*She sighs.*) Look, I'm proud of you that you have goals and ambitions. I'm…jealous of that about you, if I'm being honest. I have dreams and goals and plans too, but I just--I can't seem to make them happen like you do. One of my dreams, by the way, that I've had since you were a baby, was helping my daughter get ready for prom. (*A moment*) I also kind of dreamed that you'd do something just a little illegal at prom and I'd get to pick you up in the middle of the night in your prom dress, but I gave up on that dream a long time ago. (*Beat*) I want you to have goals. But not if it's to the exclusion of actually enjoying your life. The best parts of your life are the times when you…drive to Santa Monica with no plan and just see what happens.

(*Beat*)

ELLIE: Have no plan and just see what happens. Good advice, I'll follow it tonight. Goodbye. (*She heads for the door.*)

CLAIRE: Ellie, I know about tonight. About the hotel room. I know.

ELLIE: Well…who cares? What is your problem?! You *just* told me to let loose and have fun! I thought this would be the one time it would be awesome to have the cool mom who'd tell me to go for it! And then when I do, you freak out! I don't get you!

CLAIRE: I don't get me either! I don't know what's happening to me! I thought I'd be the cool mom too, but it turns out, when it comes right down to it, I'm just as lame as all the other moms and I'm terrified for you. *(Beat)* I know you think you're grown up—more grown up than me. And you know what, in a lot of ways you *are*. But you said you don't want your life to turn out like mine—then that means you've got to make different choices than I made.

(There's a knock on the door.)

ELLIE: Liam's here.

(ELLIE crosses and opens the door, and LIAM enters, dressed in a tux. For the first time, he looks surprisingly handsome.)

LIAM: Hey, Ellie.

ELLIE: Hey, Liam. Wow, you look…great.

LIAM: Thanks. You look…big. Your hair, I mean.

ELLIE: Oh, um…thanks.

CLAIRE: *(Under her breath)* Yikes. *(Speaking up)* Hi, I'm Claire. Ellie's mom. Let me get a picture of the two of you.

ELLIE: Moooom…

CLAIRE: It's prom! I have to take your picture on prom! Let me have this one thing!

(ELLIE *and* LIAM *stand together a little awkwardly, trying several different hand positions until they land on a very unnatural one.*)

CLAIRE: Well…that's…do you want to…you know what, I'll count to three. One, two, three!

(CLAIRE *takes the photo, and* ELLIE *and* LIAM *spring apart with relief.*)

LIAM: Should we go?

ELLIE: Yes, let's. Bye, mom.

CLAIRE: Bye. I hope you two have a really fun night. I really do. (*Beat*) And that you're careful and make smart choices, yeah? Ellie?

(*A moment as* ELLIE *looks at* CLAIRE. *She looks like she would like to turn back and hug her, or ask for advice, but she can't.*)

ELLIE: Yeah.

(ELLIE *and* LIAM *exit.*)

Scene Thirteen

(*That night, after prom. A disheveled hotel room. The bed is unmade, and there are empty beer cans littered around the room.* LIAM *and* ELLIE *enter.*)

ELLIE: Yikes. I guess Jed and some people were already in here.

(LIAM *wanders over and straightens out the bed so there's a place to sit.*)

LIAM: Do you…want to watch some TV?

ELLIE: No thanks. Do you…want to sit down?

LIAM: (*Strained*) Okay.

(LIAM *sits on the bed, and* ELLIE *sits next to him. An awkward moment.*)

ELLIE: I thought the decorations at the dance were really—

(LIAM *suddenly lunges over and kisses her. It's an aggressive kiss that knocks her back on the bed, and the two flail, unsure what to do with their hands. It's as if they are trying to recreate something they've seen in a movie, but have no idea what to do. It's painfully awkward. Suddenly* ELLIE *sits up forcefully, knocking* LIAM *off the bed and to the floor.*)

ELLIE: I have to make smart choices! I don't want to do this!

LIAM: Oh thank God, I don't want to do this either!

(LIAM *sits on the floor, leaning back against the bed. He puts his head in his hands.*)

ELLIE: I'm sorry. I know it's prom, and we're supposed to…in this nasty room…but I don't want to and…I'm so tired of feeling like I have to do things I don't want to do. (*Beat*) I'm sorry, that was rude. It's not that I don't want to…do…you…

(ELLIE *slides off the bed and sits on the ground next to him.*)

LIAM: I get it. I…feel the same way.

(LIAM *buries his head in his arms, clearly really upset.*)

ELLIE: Oh, don't be upset. It's not you. I just—

LIAM: It's not that.

ELLIE: What is it?

(*Beat*)

LIAM: My mom called this morning. She and my dad are getting divorced.

ELLIE: Oh, Liam. I'm so sorry.

LIAM: I kind of suspected it. That's why they were so insistent I do this study abroad thing. My last semester of high school. In *Indiana*. So I wouldn't be there for all of it, and they could just call me when it was done. *(He buries his face again.)* They didn't even have the balls to sit me down and look me in the face. They had to ship me to another country, and then *call* me. Cowards.

(ELLIE scoots over and puts her arm around LIAM. A moment)

LIAM: And I feel so dumb. Like, I'm graduating next month. I'm going to university. It's not like I'll still live with them. It won't really affect my life, so I don't get why I'm so upset about it.

ELLIE: I don't think you're dumb. I'd be upset too. It's a big deal.

LIAM: Thanks. *(He takes a moment to compose himself.)* I don't even want to go to university next year. I kind of just wanted to get a job and have one more year at home.

ELLIE: Really?

LIAM: Guess that's not an option anymore. And now I'll have to…why do you have to move out when you're eighteen? Says who? *(A moment)* I just…I feel like I'm like, in a river. And it's moving fast and sweeping me along and I have no control over what happens or where I'm heading. And I want to get out of the river, but it's too strong and I don't know how.

(ELLIE chuckles.)

LIAM: I'm sure that sounds stupid to you.

ELLIE: No, I was just thinking I didn't know you were capable of talking this much.

(LIAM laughs.)

LIAM: Yeah. Turns out when you're constantly afraid you're going to burst into tears, you don't talk much.

ELLIE: I don't think I realized it until you put it like that—with the river--but…that's exactly how I feel too.

LIAM: Whatever. You're like, the river guide driving the boat.

ELLIE: That's what everyone thinks. Can I tell you something?

LIAM: Sure.

ELLIE: I…kind of don't want to go to college next year either.

LIAM: For real?

ELLIE: I said "kind of" to soften it, but I definitely don't. I know I'm supposed to, and everyone expects me to. Even I expect me to.

LIAM: What do you want to do?

(*A moment*)

ELLIE: You're going to think this is so dumb.

LIAM: Um, hi, I just cried all over you. "Dumb" is taken this evening.

(ELLIE *laughs.*)

ELLIE: I have this…um…secret dream. I've never told anyone about it.

LIAM: Okay. You can tell me, if you want. You don't have to.

ELLIE: There's this elephant sanctuary in Thailand. You can go and volunteer, and you feed and bathe the elephants, and give them medicine, and help rehabilitate the ones that got hurt in the wild. And some of the work doesn't even involve hanging out with elephants—you'd be cleaning out stalls and preparing food and helping raise money to feed them.

And I just feel like…excited and wistful when I think about it.

LIAM: Wistful?

ELLIE: Sometimes I look at their website and I feel like I'm an old woman, and I feel so sad and regretful that I never went. Because like…I'm not going to do it.

LIAM: What?! Ellie you have to do it.

ELLIE: It will throw off my whole plan. And like, what if I love it? What if I get there and I love it and I never want to come back?

LIAM: Wait, wait, wait. You're not going to do it because you're afraid it will make you *too* happy?

ELLIE: But…people expect—

LIAM: Who cares? Who cares what people expect? They don't have to live your life—you do.

ELLIE: Well, yeah, but—

LIAM: All these "people" that you think are expecting you do great things will forget about you ten minutes after you fly to Thailand. Everyone is just thinking about themselves. You have to do what *you* want. *(Beat)* Like, maybe if my mom had done her own thing and waited to get married and have kids until it was something she really *wanted* to do, and not something she was *supposed* to do, my parents wouldn't be getting divorced right now.

(ELLIE *leans over and rests her head on* LIAM's *shoulder.*)

ELLIE: Thanks, Liam. I'm really sorry about your parents.

LIAM: Thanks. *(Beat)* This was the best part of prom. Just sitting here talking to you. You're really easy to talk to.

ELLIE: So are you, it turns out.

LIAM: And you're like, really nice.

ELLIE: Thanks.

(*A moment.* LIAM *leans over and kisses her—a nice, gentle kiss, not like the first one. He pulls away, a little breathless.*)

LIAM: Hey…maybe we should get married.

(ELLIE'*s breath catches.*)

LIAM: Ha, I'm totally kidding! It's a joke!

(ELLIE *laughs.* LIAM *laughs, pauses, turns to face her.*)

LIAM: Maybe we should, though. I get you. You get me. I don't mean get married right now, obviously. But like…someday. When we want to.

ELLIE: Are you serious?

LIAM: I could move to Thailand. Or we could move to Ottowa and get a bunch of dogs and celebrate Canada day. And like…we would have some assurance that we won't be alone. What do you think? Do you want to get married?

(*A long moment—this is everything* ELLIE *has been waiting for.*)

ELLIE: No. (*She gives a small laugh of disbelief.*) No. I don't think we should.

LIAM: O…kay then. Double rejected. Triple, if you count the divorce. It's a good day for Liam.

ELLIE: No, I just mean…I don't know what I want yet. And you don't either. And until we do, I don't want to make any more plans.

LIAM: Yeah, that was stupid. I'm sorry. It's been an emotional day. It just felt nice not to feel alone for a minute.

ELLIE: You don't have to be alone. Let's stay friends and…see where life takes us.

(LIAM *extends his hand.*)

LIAM: Friends?

ELLIE: *(Taking his hand)* Friends.

(There is a knock at the door. LIAM stands and opens it, and a police OFFICER stands outside.)

LIAM: *(Nervously)* Yes, officer?

OFFICER: I'm looking for Ian Atkinson.

(LIAM lets out a sigh of relief.)

LIAM: Oh, that's not me.

OFFICER: Well then, that's a problem. This room was booked with his credit card and he's reported it stolen.

ELLIE: Oh, no, his son booked the rooms! Jed Atkinson?

OFFICER: *(To LIAM)* Are you Jed Atkinson?

LIAM: *(Again, relieved)* No, I'm not.

OFFICER: Well, then that's a problem. Either way, you're in a room that's been booked with a stolen credit card. *(She glances in the room.)* You been drinking tonight?

ELLIE: No! No, no, no! Those were there when we got here! We're underage.

(LIAM shoots her an "are you an idiot?" look.)

OFFICER: Mmm-hmm. I'm going to need you to come with me. Let's go.

ELLIE/LIAM: What?/Are you serious?!

(The OFFICER enters the room and rounds ELLIE and LIAM up, escorting them out of the room as they continue to protest.)

Scene Fourteen

(Later that evening, the hotel lobby. JANA, ELLIE, *and* LIAM *sit next to each other in chairs, waiting for their parents. The* OFFICER *stands nearby.)*

JANA: *(To* LIAM*)* And it turns out Jed is an even bigger idiot than I thought, and he was grounded and wasn't even supposed to *go* to prom, and then he booked all those rooms with his dad's credit card without telling him, and then his dad figured it out and decided Jed would get scared straight if the police knocked on his door. And *then* the police burst in and saw me in my dress and thought I was a prostitute, so that didn't help.

OFFICER: Jana? Your mom's here. Thankfully.

*(*JANA *stands up to leave.)*

JANA: Peace out, virgins!

ELLIE: Jana, God!

*(*ELLIE *rolls her eyes.* JANA *exits. The* OFFICER *calls over.)*

OFFICER: Liam? Your mom's here.

LIAM: She's not my mom.

OFFICER: Well, you can go with her or I can take you over to the police station.

*(*LIAM *springs to his feet.)*

LIAM: Great! Off I go! *(He turns to* ELLIE.*)* Hey. Thanks for a really great night.

*(*ELLIE *gestures to the POLICE* OFFICER.*)*

ELLIE: Ha, yeah, it was really great.

LIAM: I mean it. It was.

*(*ELLIE *stands up and* LIAM *gives her a hug.)*

Thanks.

(The OFFICER *escorts* LIAM *offstage, and passes* CLAIRE *as she enters.)*

OFFICER: That one yours?

CLAIRE: Yep.

OFFICER: You can take her.

(The OFFICER *and* LIAM *exit, and* CLAIRE *enters and sits next to* ELLIE. *She is trying very hard to withhold a smile, but glee is bursting through and she can't help herself. A moment.)*

CLAIRE: I'm so happy.

ELLIE: *(Also trying not to smile)* Okay.

CLAIRE: I had two dreams for tonight, and they both came true. I got to get you ready for prom, and you got in enough trouble that I got to pick you up in the middle of the night.

ELLIE: I didn't do anything wrong. Jed—

CLAIRE: Shh, shh, shh. Just let me have this.

ELLIE: But I—

CLAIRE: I know. Jana's mom called me.

ELLIE: She was wearing the dress you picked and they thought she was a hooker.

CLAIRE: This is the best night of my life! Let's go.

ELLIE: Mom, I…um…I didn't do anything tonight.

CLAIRE: I told you, I know. Jana's mom—

ELLIE: No, like…I didn't *do* anything tonight. And I just…wanted you to know.

CLAIRE: Oh. I see.

ELLIE: I almost did. And then something came over me and I quoted you and knocked him on the floor.

CLAIRE: You quoted *me*?

ELLIE: "Make smart choices."

CLAIRE: Ah. Well, you didn't need me to tell you that.

ELLIE: Maybe. I just…um…thanks for being my mom tonight.

(CLAIRE *puts her arm around* ELLIE.)

CLAIRE: Well, I don't have many more chances. Got to get them in while I can.

ELLIE: Why? Who's dying?

CLAIRE: No, I just mean soon you'll be off at college, doing your own thing. You won't need me as much. And you didn't need me all that much to begin with, so…

ELLIE: I'll always need you.

CLAIRE: Blah blah Hallmark card, I know. I just… sometimes I wish we were elephants. They were the ones that stay with their moms their whole life, right?

ELLIE: Yeah. Some of them do.

CLAIRE: That's nice for those mom elephants. They don't ever have to be alone. (*She stands up to leave.*)

ELLIE: You okay?

CLAIRE: I'm fulfilling my lifelong dream of picking my delinquent daughter up on prom night. I'm great!

(*Beat*)

ELLIE: What did you mean earlier tonight? About being jealous of me, because you can't seem to make your dreams happen?

CLAIRE: Nothing. It was in the heat of an argument.

ELLIE: Mom.

(*Beat.* CLAIRE *sits back down.*)

CLAIRE: I just meant…you make a lot of comments about how terrible my life decision are, and…

ELLIE: I'm sorry. I'm sorry I said that…that I've *been* saying that.

CLAIRE: When I was your age I had a lot of plans for my life too, but life had different plans for me. And now…I don't know. *You've* been my life. My entire adult life, and I've loved every moment of it. And that chapter is ending and…I'm not old. But I'm not young. And I feel a little…lost. I should probably get that puppy.

ELLIE: On the one hand there is no way on earth that you should get that puppy. On the other hand, I really want you to get it so you have something to hold you down.

CLAIRE: Hold me down?

ELLIE: I'm like…worried about you. When I leave. Right now, if you meet some loser and he's like "let's go bungee jump off the Sears tower," you have to say no because you have to come home to me. When I'm gone, I don't know what's going to keep you from going totally off the deep end. *(A long moment)* What was your plan? Before me?

CLAIRE: My plan was Chicago too, actually. I was going to go to the Art Institute of Chicago.

ELLIE: You applied?

CLAIRE: I got in.

ELLIE: You did?!

CLAIRE: Yes, I did! Just because you don't like the stuff I make doesn't mean other people don't!

ELLIE: Mom, you should go.

CLAIRE: Oh, please.

ELLIE: Why not? Maybe your dream just got deferred for a little while. What's to stop you now?

CLAIRE: I'm thirty-seven. I'd be twice as old as everyone there.

ELLIE: Only on the outside. On the inside, I think you'll fit right in. Mom, I *really* think you should go.

CLAIRE: I could never afford it.

ELLIE: There are so many scholarships for old peop— for adult students who want to go to college. I've been applying to scholarships for years. I'm a master. I can help you.

(*A moment as* CLAIRE *actually entertains the idea.*)

CLAIRE: Really?

ELLIE: Yes! This could be your next chapter!

CLAIRE: And I could like, get an apartment in Chicago. And go to Cubs games. And sketch on Navy Pier.

ELLIE: Yeah!

CLAIRE: And we could like, have brunch on Sundays!

(ELLIE *shifts uncomfortably.*)

CLAIRE: Or you can pretend that your lame mom didn't follow you to Chicago and we'll never have to see each other.

ELLIE: No, it's not that. I…um…oh boy.

CLAIRE: What?

ELLIE: I'm…thinking of not going to college next year.

(CLAIRE *teasingly calls out to the police officer.*)

CLAIRE: Excuse me, officer, my daughter's been abducted!

ELLIE: Stop! I know, I know. I just…I've had this picture of what my life was supposed to be, and I've felt like, crushed under that picture for a long time. And tonight I had the chance to check part of it off the list, and…I didn't want it. I don't know if I want any of it. I might want to throw that picture out and make a new one.

(A moment)

CLAIRE: And…would that picture look anything like an elephant hospital?

ELLIE: Sanctuary! What?! How did you know that?

CLAIRE: Good moms check your internet history.

ELLIE: *What?!*

CLAIRE: I love you; you're welcome. You visit that page almost every day.

ELLIE: Okay, well…officially I'm mad at you…but… what do you think?

CLAIRE: It's *me*. What do you think I think?! It's what you really want, and you should do it.

ELLIE: Really?

CLAIRE: Really. That's all I've ever wanted for you. College will be there. Or not. I think when you're young you should choose the biggest, most exciting option you have. Later in life you might not be able to.

ELLIE: Ha, you still do.

CLAIRE: I'm still young, right? *(She winks.)* You know, I feel really good about this. All of it. About Chicago. About the elephant church.

ELLIE: *(Laughing)* Sanctuary. So do I.

CLAIRE: Want to go get some breakfast?

ELLIE: It's three AM. I'm in a prom dress. *(A moment)* Yes, yes I do.

(ELLIE hugs CLAIRE, and the two exit with their arms around each other.)

Scene Fifteen

(Two weeks later, school. The Living History exhibit. There are two small platforms for JANA *and* ELLIE *to stand on, and a microphone set up stage left for* MRS SPEARE *to make announcements. Three chairs are also stage right for the "audience" of* CLAIRE, MRS SPEARE, *and* LIAM. MRS SPEARE *approaches the microphone.)*

MRS SPEARE: Good afternoon, everyone, and welcome to the final round of the Living History exhibit! For those of you who were with us for the talent portion, welcome back! For those of you just joining us, the students in today's exhibit are from my senior history class, and have been working on this project all semester. Each student was to choose an influential person that they admire, research them, design a costume, and put together a presentation that gives us some insight into that person's significance in history and personal philosophies. Today's presentation is special, because not only is it their final project for the semester, but the winner will be receiving a scholarship from the Indiana Historical Society. Those of you who were here at the earlier rounds heard from such influential people as Abraham Lincoln, Sally Ride, and… *(She sighs deeply.)* Alec Baldwin. Contestants are being judged based on written papers they turned in before the competition, and on all three in-person rounds: Costume, Talent, and our final round, the Interview. Only two ladies have made it to the final round, and it's an interesting pairing, if I do say so myself—Eleanor Roosevelt and Dolly Parton!

(She takes her seat as she, CLAIRE, *and* LIAM *applaud.* JANA, *dressed extravagantly as Dolly Parton, and* ELLIE, *dressed conservatively as Eleanor Roosevelt, enter, competitively elbowing each other out of the way as they walk to their platforms.* JANA *speaks with Dolly's high pitched country*

twang; ELLIE *speaks with Eleanor's very proper, rounded sound.)*

JANA: Well howdy, ya'll! I'm just pleased as punch to see ya!

ELLIE: Warmest greetings, my beloved fellow Americans.

MRS SPEARE: Ladies, I will be asking you a series of questions. You will have one minute to respond, and when your time is up, you will hear this bell. *(She dings a little bell on a table in front of her.)* First question: Please give us a brief introduction on who you are, and your educational background.

(A screen behind them lights up with the words "Introduction and Education".)

MRS SPEARE: Ms Roosevelt, you will begin.

ELLIE: While I was originally known for being the longest-serving First Lady, I went on to have my own career as a politician, activist, and diplomat. I was born in New York to a wealthy, upwardly-mobile family— my uncle was Teddy Roosevelt. I was educated in London and at the best private boarding schools.

JANA: As for me, I guess there are two things I'm really well known for. *(She looks down at her bosom.)* My songs and my philanthropy. You see, I was born in a tiny backwoods house in Tennessee, with eleven brothers and sisters! We didn't have running water or electricity, and we were poor as church mice. But I wanted to know, I had to know, that you can come from nothin'—don't have to be educated, don't have to be rich or sophisticated—and still make somethin' of your life.

MRS SPEARE: Thank you. Next question: What is your philosophy on success?

(The screen reads "Philosophy on Success".)

ELLIE: When people ask me about my success, I tell them that I believe the only important ingredients are curiosity, interest, imagination, and a sense of the adventure of life.

(*She smiles at* CLAIRE *in the audience, who smiles back.* JANA *looks a little surprised by* ELLIE'*s answer.*)

JANA: Well, shoot, you sound like a lady I'd like to get a beer with, Ms Roosevelt. When people ask me about *my* success, and my philosophy, I tell them--I am a list maker. I like to write my goals and plans down and keep them in a secret place where people can't see them. If there is something I really want, I write it down on a piece of paper and I look at the list and I concentrate real hard on it, try to visualize it happening, and I just go through all the motions as if it's already done.

(ELLIE *breaks character, surprised by this information.*)

ELLIE: Really?

JANA: (*With a small shrug and smile, as herself*) Yeah.

(MRS SPEARE *dings the bell.*)

MRS SPEARE: Contestants, please refrain from speaking to each other.

JANA: Well, that ain't friendly.

CLAIRE: Next question: What is your outlook on physical appearance?

(*The screen reads "Physical Appearance".*)

ELLIE: (*As herself*) Hold on. Was that going to be one of the questions if two *men* made it to the finals?!

JANA: (*As Dolly*) This is some bullshit, ma'am.

MRS SPEARE: Ladies! The clock is running.

ELLIE: I'm just saying, you wouldn't have asked Abraham Lincoln that question.

(ELLIE *and* JANA *both roll their eyes, then smile a little at their similar reaction.* ELLIE *gets back into her Eleanor character.*)

ELLIE: When I was very young, maybe five, my mother started calling me "granny", because she thought I looked so old fashioned. I hated that.

(ELLIE *and* JANA *exchange a look;* JANA *looks remorseful.*)

ELLIE: It started a life-long battle between the way I looked, and the way other people wished I looked— the way I wished I looked. But no matter how plain a woman may be, if truth and loyalty are stamped upon her face, all will be attracted to her.

JANA: I agree with you, Ms Roosevelt, but I took a little bit of a different approach to my look—it may be what I'm best known for! I'm a totally different person from the way I look. I really am. Can you imagine anybody wanting to look this way for real? But why not? Life's boring enough, it makes you try to spice it up. But there's a brain beneath the wigs and a heart beneath the boobs.

(*The bell dings.*)

MRS SPEARE: Please tell us about your marriages and home life.

(*The screen reads "Marriage and Home Life".*)

ELLIE: I married Franklin, who was my fifth cousin. We had six children together, and while our marriage was not always a happy…or faithful…one, we were intellectual equals who pushed each other on.

JANA: I met my husband, Carl Dean, the day I moved to Nashville. He whistled at me out the side of his car while I was at a laundromat, and we've been together ever since! He hates the limelight, so he stays home in Tennessee while I galivant the world. We don't have any kids, and we're just as happy as can be with our little arrangement, even if the rest of the world doesn't get it. There have even been rumors that I'm a lesbian!

ELLIE: Me too!

JANA: *(Acting shocked)* Really! Mine are about me and my secretary, Judy. You?

ELLIE: Amelia Earhart.

(JANA *playfully throws up her hands.)*

JANA: You win!

(MRS SPEARE *dings the bell)*

MRS SPEARE: Ooooook. Moving forward to our last question. Please describe the accomplishments of which you are most proud.

(The screen reads "Accomplishments".)

JANA: I'm real proud of my career as a singer, songwriter, actress, and businesswoman. But I'm prouder of the work I've done to help people. One of the things I'm real proud of is my amusement park, Dollywood. That's been one of the dreams of my life—to be able to go back home to do something great for that part of the country.

ELLIE: Well put, Ms Parton. While I'm of course also proud of the *numerous* awards I received throughout my life, I'm most proud of the work I did to help people. I'm very proud of founding Val-Kill Industries in my hometown in New York, which provided jobs and incomes for many, many local families, and paved the way for my husband's New Deal.

(JANA *gives* ELLIE *a look, surprised by the similarity. But she'd also like to one-up her. The bell dings.)*

MRS SPEARE: Thank you. And—

JANA: We also have what we call the Dollywood Foundation—we focus mostly on the education of

the kids. We work very hard to give scholarships
to struggling kids, and we have a hotline to the
Dollywood Foundation in case they get in trouble.

(ELLIE *is also surprised by Dolly's accomplishment, but can
play this game. It's on.*)

ELLIE: I was of course honored to be appointed to the
United Nations, where I helped pen the Universal
Declaration of Human Rights.

(JANA *has more ammo.* MRS SPEARE *rings the bell again.*)

MRS SPEARE: Ladies, time is up—

JANA: I'm also real proud of my Imagination Library.
Every kid in Sevier County gets a book a month from
the day it's born until the day it starts kindergarten.

(*But wait,* ELLIE *also has more ammo.*)

ELLIE: Of course, I was also instrumental in founding
the National Youth Administration, which provided
education and job training for four million young
people during the Great Depression.

(*The competition ramps up as* MRS SPEARE *dings again.*)

MRS SPEARE: Ladies—

JANA: I've written over three thousand songs.

ELLIE: I've written seventy-eight books.

JANA: I've received nineteen honorary degrees.

ELLIE: And I've received thirty-five.

JANA: Well, if you're ever in California, Ms Roosevelt,
you can visit my *two* stars on the Hollywood Walk of
Fame.

ELLIE: And you can visit my National Historic Site in
New York.

(MRS SPEARE *frantically dings the bell multiple times and
stands up, momentarily losing her cool.*)

MRS SPEARE: TIME'S UP! (*A moment as she regains her composure and smiles at the audience.*) Oooook, that was great. Let's give a big round of applause for Dolly Parton and Eleanor Roosevelt!

(MRS SPEARE *leads* CLAIRE, LIAM, *and the audience in applause.*)

MRS SPEARE: Contestants, if you will please wait offstage, the judges will deliberate about the winner of today's contest, and the recipient of the scholarship!

(ELLIE *hops of her platform and takes off her wig.*)

ELLIE: Oh, wait, Mrs Speare, can I say something?

MRS SPEARE: Um…I guess so.

ELLIE: I just wanted…maybe this is cheesy, but I wanted to thank my mom for helping me with this project. For helping me see Eleanor Roosevelt in a new way. Eleanor was all about embracing the adventure of life, and my mom's been teaching me that since I was born. I…I almost changed my mind and did my mom for this project, but then I thought she might get mad if I did her for a history exhibit.

(*All eyes are on* CLAIRE, *and she half-stands with a small smile.*)

CLAIRE: I'm thirty-seven.

ELLIE: But I could have done her, because she's someone I admire. Thanks.

MRS SPEARE: Thank you, Ellie. Contestants, please wait offstage.

(ELLIE *and* JANA *cross stage right, taking off their wigs;* JANA *takes out her balloon boobs.*)

ELLIE: You did really great out there. Like, *really* great.

JANA: You too. Not that anyone's surprised by that.

ELLIE: I…um…I didn't know any of that about Dolly Parton. I knew she was a singer with big boobs, but that was it. She's like…kind of awesome. *(Beat)* Is it me, or are the like…kind of the same?

JANA: That's what I thought! I was standing on that platform thinking, "These badass bitches were both kicking ass and taking names, and just doing it in like, totally different ways."

(A moment)

ELLIE: Jana, I'm sorry.

JANA: No, I'm sorry!

(ELLIE and JANA try to hug, but JANA's balloon boobs are in the way. They laugh.)

ELLIE: I was just jealous, and—

JANA: I've been exhibiting so many un-Dollylike qualities! And I missed you!

ELLIE: I missed you too! And I *was* being a judgmental bitch! I'm sorry! Guess what.

JANA: What?

ELLIE: Liam asked me to marry him.

JANA: Whaaaaaa?! Stop it! Are you kidding me?! WE DID IT! *(She leaps and does a series of elated dance moves.)* You're engaged?!

ELLIE: *(Smiling)* I said no.

JANA: You said no.

ELLIE: I said no.

JANA: Gaaaaaaah! What have we been doing for the last month?! This was going to be the one thing I accomplished before my mom has me killed for being almost arrested on fake prostitution charges. And now I've accomplished nothing.

ELLIE: I wouldn't say that.

MRS SPEARE: Ladies and gentlemen, our judges have deliberated, and we'd like to welcome our two finalists to the stage. Ellie Hoyt and Jana Meyers!

(ELLIE *and* JANA *look at each other with surprise. They throw their wigs back on,* JANA *stuffs her balloons back in, and they head center stage.*)

MRS SPEARE: Ladies, the judges would like to congratulate you on your stellar performances today, and for showing us two very different women who impacted the world. But there can only be one scholarship winner, and that winner is…Jana Meyers!

(JANA *looks completely shocked.* ELLIE *is thrilled, and throws her arms around* JANA *in a fierce hug. The hug pops one [or both?] of* JANA's *balloon boobs, and the audience screams and ducks for cover.*)

JANA: It's okay, it's okay everyone…it's just my boobs! (*She soaks in her moment, and throws her arms in the air.*) My prize-winning boobs!

(JANA, ELLIE, MRS SPEARE, *and the rest of the "audience" leave in celebration.* LIAM *hangs back and stands alone awkwardly;* CLAIRE *approaches him.*)

CLAIRE: Hey, Liam.

LIAM: Hi, Ms Hoyt.

(*A moment. They don't have much to say to each other.*)

CLAIRE: (*Playfully*) So…what are your intentions with my daughter?

LIAM: Oh, I, um, I didn't mean any—

CLAIRE: I'm kidding, I'm kidding. Unclench.

LIAM: Sorry Ellie didn't win. And that she told everyone your age.

CLAIRE: Nah, Jana and those boobs earned it. I think Ellie has other plans anyway.

LIAM: Yeah, the elephants. She told me. She's lucky she knows what she wants to do.

CLAIRE: What about you? What are your plans after school ends?

LIAM: I don't really know. I feel a little lost going back home, I guess.

CLAIRE: I hear that. But you know what? I think maybe you found who you are here. What if you took him home with you? And into your future?

(Something sinks in for LIAM, *and he gives a small smile.* CLAIRE *returns his smile, gives him a squeeze on the arm, and exits.)*

Scene Sixteen

(Two months later. Outside the airport. LIAM, ELLIE, *and* CLAIRE *stand with backpacks and rolling luggage.* JANA *stands with them, with just her purse. We can hear boarding announcements and other airport sounds in the background.)*

ELLIE: Thanks for the ride, Jana. We appreciate it— we'd never fit in mom's car with all her stuff for Chicago.

JANA: It's cool. Even though you're all leaving me, and the last thing you did was ask me for a favor. It's cool.

ELLIE: This is weird. Like, we're all here right now, and we're all going to go to bed in totally different parts of the world tonight. Canada, Chicago, Thailand…

JANA: Here.

CLAIRE: But going to college for *free*.

JANA: Community college. But just until I can take enough classes to figure out what I want to do. Then I'm gonna transfer somewhere awesome.

CLAIRE: I know you are.

(CLAIRE *gives her a little hug, and* LIAM *crosses to* ELLIE.)

LIAM: Well…we'll be in touch, right?

ELLIE: Right. Let me know how things go with your parents.

LIAM: Thanks. For everything. I hope we see each other again someday.

ELLIE: Well, no matter what, we'll always have room 206.

(LIAM *laughs. They hug, and* JANA *crosses to them and breaks it up.*)

JANA: Hey, milk-bag, stop hogging my best friend.

(JANA *gives* LIAM *a playful shove and he laughs.* LIAM *crosses over to chat with* CLAIRE.)

JANA: So…this sucks. I'm going to miss you.

ELLIE: I'm going to miss you too. You'd better text me every day. I want to know every awesome thing you're doing.

JANA: You know I will. You'd better save all the elephants. Like, all fifty species.

ELLIE: Actually, there are only three species of elephants, and they—

JANA: Ugh, never mind, I don't miss you anymore. Go.

(ELLIE *laughs, and the two give each other a fierce hug.* JANA *crosses over to* LIAM, *and* ELLIE *crosses to* CLAIRE.)

CLAIRE: You let me know the second you land.

ELLIE: I will. You better drive safe and send me pictures of your new place. (*She is a little emotional.*)

CLAIRE: Hey. I'm going to come visit you on my Thanksgiving break.

ELLIE: And I'm going to come see you at Christmas.

(CLAIRE *nods, also a little emotional.*)

ELLIE: Oh, I got you something! (*She reaches in her bag and pulls out a stuffed elephant.*) So the mama elephant is never alone.

CLAIRE: Shut up!

ELLIE: I…thought that would be touching, but whatever.

(CLAIRE *reaches in her purse and pulls out a small, beaded elephant.* ELLIE *bursts out laughing.*)

ELLIE: No way!

CLAIRE: I made it. So you always have your mama elephant.

(CLAIRE *and* ELLIE *exchange elephants.*)

CLAIRE: I'm really, really proud of you.

ELLIE: I'm proud of you too, mom.

(CLAIRE *and* ELLIE *hug fiercely.*)

CLAIRE: Okay, international travelers. You two better go so you can get though security in time. And I've gotta hit the road. Everybody ready?

(*A moment as each person looks straight forward, as if looking at the future they've chosen for themselves.*)

ELLIE: Ready.

LIAM: Me too.

JANA: Same.

CLAIRE: Then let's do this.

(The four come together in a group hug, then split to exit different directions, turning to give each other last looks. ELLIE takes a breath, with a smile, center stage.)

END OF PLAY